the handmade book

angela james

photography by emma peios

The mission of Storey Communications is to serve our customers by publishing practical information that encourages personal independence in harmony with the environment.

North American edition published in 2000 by Storey Books,
Schoolhouse Road, Pownal, Vermont 05261
United Kingdom edition published in 2000 by New Holland Publishers (UK) Ltd,
24 Nutford Place, London W1H 6DQ

10 9 8 7 6 5 4 3 2 1

ISBN 1 58017 256 3

Editor: Christine Rista
Assistant Editor: Kate Latham
Design and Art Direction: Blackjacks
Photographer: Emma Peios
Editorial Direction: Rosemary Wilkinson

Reproduction by Modern Age Repro House Ltd., Hong Kong
Printed and bound in Singapore by Tien Wah Press (Pte) Ltd

Library of Congress Cataloging-in-Publication Data

James, Angela.
    The handmade book / Angela James ; photography by Emma Peios.
       p.   cm.
    Includes bibliographical references.
    ISBN 1-58017-256-3
    1. Bookbinding--Amateurs' manuals. I. Peios, Emma. II. Title.

Z266 .J36 2000
686.3--dc21

99 056192

contents

introd

Handmade books have always been regarded as something special, and in this age of information technology and the impersonality of so much printed material, they are even more treasured.

The techniques of bookbinding have changed little over time. If I were to bring a binder from two or three centuries ago into my workshop, he (and it would have been a he) would feel quite at home in his surroundings; certainly he would recognize most of the tools and equipment. That said, bookbinding is by no means stuck in the past. Far from the word processor and the Internet heralding the demise of the book, you have only to look around you at the number of flourishing bookshops to realize that reading continues to be an important part of many people's lives. The book as an object is uniquely satisfying, and the outer cover is a crucial component of the package. Hand-bound books continue to be in great demand as memorial books, portfolios, guest books, and so on. In the following pages I hope to demonstrate that bookbinding is still very much alive in the 21st century.

I have divided this book into three sections. The first covers materials, tools and techniques; the second comprises 13 step-by-step projects with photographs; and the third section shows contemporary book bindings.

The bindings shown in this last section are one-of-a-kind, largely commissioned by private collectors, or for public collections. They are the result of years of training and many hours of work, but do not let that discourage you. All bookbinders have to start with the basics at the beginning of their career.

The step-by-step projects are more realistic ambitions for beginners. Before you start, though, read the section on materials, tools and techniques. In the materials section, all the materials used in the projects are listed, and, in some cases, alternatives are suggested. Most items will be available from good art shops, but there is also a list of specialist suppliers on page 78. There is a wealth of choice: papers come in all the colors of the spectrum; thick and thin; rough and smooth. Some papers contain leaves and petals; some are printed, others marbled, handmade, machine-made or recycled. Then there are the bookcloths in their various textures and colors, leathers and suedes of all kinds, fabrics of the widest possible variety, plastics, wood, even metal.

All the tools needed are explained in the section on tools, and the few which are not readily available from a hardware store or an art shop can be bought from bookbinding suppliers.

The section on techniques lists a few dos and don'ts. Read these before you start — it will repay you to follow them carefully, and familiarize yourself with certain basics, which with practice will become second nature.

I am often asked how I came to be a bookbinder: the answer is partly "being in the right place at the right time." At art school I specialized in printed textile design, but chose bookbinding as my subsidiary subject, mainly because no one else was doing it. I soon became absorbed, partly thanks to the delightful elderly man who taught me, and partly because designing and making a book satisfies both the creative side of my nature and the pleasure I derive from precise and careful work — in other words, craftsmanship. On graduating, I chose to pursue bookbinding rather than textile design, and was fortunate to find work and training in one of the few craft workshops in Britain. I worked there for some time, and eventually felt qualified to set up my own bindery. The pleasure and satisfaction I take in my work have never diminished, and I hope this book will inspire you to explore this wonderful craft beyond these pages.

Angela James

uction

tools for bookmaking

Bookbinding requires a few specialty tools, but most of what you need initially is readily available from hardware stores or ordinary art shops. Once you have these essentials you can build up your collection gradually as your skills improve.

BONE FOLDER: Bone folders come in two sizes and can be bought at bookbinding suppliers. One about 100 mm (4 in) long is suitable.

AWL AND PIN: These are tools for making holes or for marking. The awl can be bought in a toolshop, and the pin can be made by taking a thick needle, such as a bookbinders' needle, and fixing it into a short length of dowel with a hole drilled through the top of it.

BRUSHES: Brushes can be bought from bookbinding suppliers, art shops or from hardware stores. For glueing jobs you will need a 40 mm (1½ in) brush and a larger one for glueing large areas. A smaller brush is useful for more precise jobs, and you will also want a watercolor brush (number 6 or 7) for painting the edges of boards.

CARPENTER'S SQUARE, CHISEL, HAMMER AND SAW: All these can be found in toolshops. The chisels must be of the same width as your ribbons; the hammer and saw can be general-purpose ones.

CUTTING MAT: A self-healing cutting mat is used for every project in this book. Buy one measuring at least 450 x 300 mm (18 x 12 in).

DIVIDERS: Dividers are used for all kinds of measuring and marking. A pair about 150 mm (6 in) long is ideal.

DRILL: This is needed for two of the projects. A hand drill and a set of drill bits can be bought at any toolshop.

C-CLAMP: This is used to secure boards to the table while plaiting threads or drilling holes.

KNIVES: A heavy craft knife with replaceable blades is essential for cutting board and paper. Smaller craft knives can be used for lighter jobs, but not for cutting chipboard.

PENCILS AND ERASERS: A general-purpose HB pencil is suitable, and also a soft pencil that can be easily rubbed out, for example a 3B or 4B.

PRESSING BOARDS: These can be made from plywood of at least 3 ply; 5 ply is better. They should be at least 450 x 300 mm (18 x 12 in), and you need a pair. Be sure to sand the edges of the boards well after cutting the boards to size, as there will be many splinters.

PUNCHES: Available from specialty toolmakers, they are useful for making small holes but are not essential.

RULER AND STRAIGHT-EDGE: You need a ruler at least 300 mm (12 in) long, showing both metric and imperial measurements, and a steel straight-edge with a non-slip backing of at least 500 mm (20 in).

SCISSORS: Two pairs are useful, one medium size and a small pair with sharp points.

SET SQUARE OR TRIANGLE: If possible, find one with 300 mm (12 in) sides. A protractor is also useful.

WEIGHTS: Weights, rather than bookbinders' presses, are used for pressing in these projects. They can be found in junk shops. Look for the type used with old-fashioned scales or old cast-iron flatirons. Alternatively, ask an engineering workshop to make some for you.

BRUSHES DIVIDERS WEIGHTS

CUTTING MAT

AWL AND PIN

BONE FOLDERS

CRAFT KNIVES

CHISELS

C-CLAMP

SAW

PUNCHES

DRILL

SET SQUARE

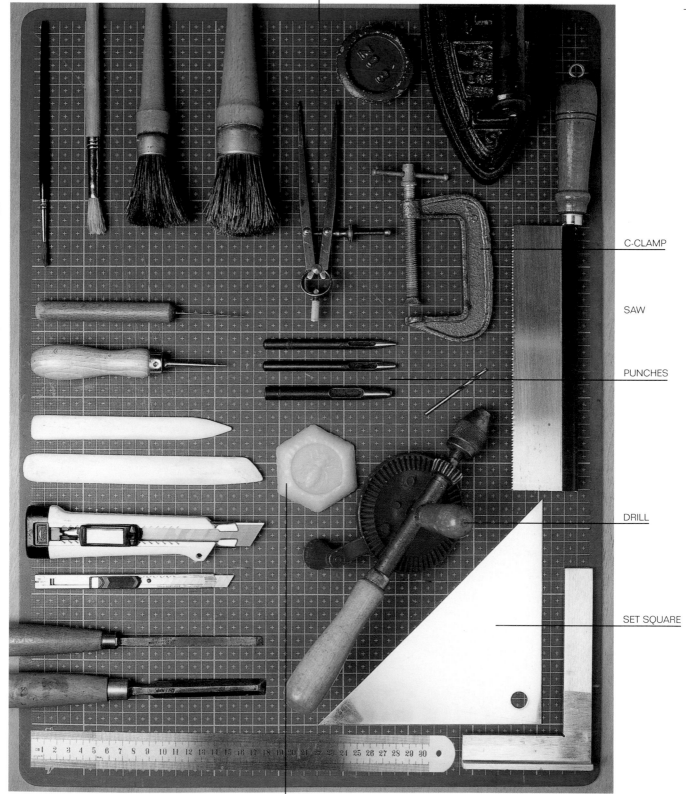

RULER/STRAIGHT-EDGE BEESWAX CARPENTER'S SQUARE

bookmaking materials

Today's binders have an unprecedented variety of materials from which to choose. The only limit, once you have mastered the basic techniques, is your imagination. Let it run, and conjure up all sorts of possibilities and, above all, enjoy your bookmaking.

ACRYLIC INKS

These inks are used for coloring paper and the edges of boards. They come in a wide range of colors and can be bought from art shops.

ADHESIVES

Polyvinyl acetate adhesive (PVA) is used for most of the books here. It can be bought from craft shops and bookbinding suppliers, as can paste, a starch-based adhesive used in two of the projects. Clear general-purpose glue is also used in two of the projects.

BEESWAX AND POLISH

Thread is drawn through a block of beeswax to give it a protective coating. Beeswax and a good natural color wax polish are both used for polishing wood.

BOARD

The board used in all the projects is chipboard — a very dense board that cuts and sands well. It is usually pH neutral and can be obtained from specialty paper and bookbinding suppliers. Strawboard should never be used; it is much too acidic and will degrade very quickly.

BOOKCLOTH

There are many bookcloths and buckrams on the market. Buckram is heavier than bookcloth and harder wearing. Both come in a variety of colors and textures and are available from bookbinding suppliers. Try to find one with an interesting texture.

FABRIC

Fabric is very useful for covering books. It has to be backed with paper, so remember to choose a fairly fine material such as cotton, linen, or silk. The latter, however, does not wear well and thus should be used only very occasionally. Other materials, such as felt, are particularly well-suited for lining the insides of portfolios.

FASTENINGS

Double-sided satin ribbon, unbleached linen tape, cords or webbing can all be used for fastenings and can be found in notions departments. Some shops specialize in buttons and beads, or you can make your own from pieces of hardwood, shell, stone or metal.

LEATHER

Leather is used in very small amounts in these projects, as paring-down leather (taking off some of the thickness with a knife and/or spoke-shave) requires fairly advanced skills. In the Leather-Bound and the Spotty Photograph Album projects, leather is used for closures and needs no paring down. As it is expensive to buy a whole skin, which you won't need for these projects, it is worth hunting in craft shops for bags of scraps, or begging left-overs from bookbinders or other leather workers.

LINEN

Linen can be bought from any good fabric store. On books it is used for lining spines and for making joints, as in the portfolio project. In the Japanese Octagon project I used jaconette, a sheer, lightweight cotton fabric, instead because it is easy to cut and frays less than linen. Usually it is much better to use a fine linen with a dense weave — sometimes described as airplane linen.

LINEN TAPES

Linen tapes can be bought unbleached from most good notions departments and also from bookbinding suppliers. They are mainly used in multi-section sewing to link the different sections together (see instructions on sewing on page 13).

PAPERS

Most papers are identified by weight, measured in grams per square meter (gsm). Machine-made papers have a grain direction (the direction in which the fibers lie). Always ensure that the grain of all papers you use, including boards, runs in the same direction. Handmade papers, which do not have a grain direction, can in themselves be an intrinsic part of the design of a book. Several kinds of paper are used in the following projects:

Text-weight paper is appropriate as text paper or as endpapers. Colored text paper can be found in specialty shops. It is supplied in various weights, but the ideal range is between 90 and 110 gsm or 60 to 70 lb.

Watercolor paper comes in several different weights and is very versatile. It is described as either HP, i.e. hot-pressed, which means it has a smooth surface; NOT, which means it has been pressed without felts and has a rougher surface; or Rough, which means it has not been pressed at all and is the most textured of the three. NOT is suitable for both cover and text, depending on the weight. HP can be used for text, and Rough for covers.

Silicone-release paper is very useful for putting between pressing boards and when rubbing down with a bone folder. No glue will stick to it. It can be bought in large sheets from specialty stores, or from kitchen shops, where it is called non-stick baking parchment.

Blotting paper is used mostly for putting between pressing boards, where it takes up any small bumps in the board that might mark the book. It is also, of course, used for blotting.

Newsprint is the paper on which newspapers are printed — confusingly, it is unprinted. Do not use actual newspaper, as the solvents in the glue will release the ink from the paper and leave dirty marks.

Paper stretches when it is wet. Thinner papers and machine-made papers stretch more than other types, and it is as well to be aware of this when glueing out and sticking down. Try to work quickly, before the dampness from the glue makes the paper stretch too much. This is less of a problem when using PVA (polyvinyl acetate adhesive), which dries faster than starch-based glues. Remember that a paper that has stretched before it is stuck down will shrink back to its former size when dry, pulling the paper or board on which it is stuck with it.

SUEDE

Suede is easy to work with and makes an ideal cover for simple bindings. It is available in a wide selection of colors but has to be bought from specialty stores (see suppliers' list on page 78).

THREADS

In most of the projects, linen thread is recommended. It is strong and durable and can be bought in any good notions department. It comes in various thicknesses, but a good general-purpose thread would be 25/2. The most commonly available color is natural, but it also comes in black, brown and khaki.

Polyester buttonhole-weight thread is used for sewing and plaiting for making fastenings. Not as strong as linen thread, but durable, it comes in most colors and can be bought from notions departments.

Silk thread comes in lovely shades and has a good lustre but is not very durable. In buttonhole-weight, it can be used for plaiting, and is not as stiff as polyester.

VELLUM

Vellum is the skin of calves or goats. It is a hard-wearing material and is usually sold in its natural color. This ranges from cream to light brown, but sometimes a skin can have darker shading from the markings on the animal. The vellum I used for the Leather-Bound book and the Italian Style binding has been dyed. Vellum is available only from specialty stores (see suppliers' list on page 78) and is very expensive.

WOOD

The boards of early printed books and manuscripts were very often wooden, and stripwood is used here to form the cover of Peter Jones's Wooden Boards book. The first project uses a wooden dowel as a spinepiece, and the maple and suede binding has a drilled maple spinepiece. Most model-making shops should have a reasonable selection of suitable woods — choose one with an interesting grain if possible, and remember to avoid anything that is too soft.

bookmaking techniques

There are several techniques that are used throughout the book. It is worthwhile familiarizing yourself with them in this section, remembering that you can refer back to the instructions here.

measuring

Careful and accurate measuring and folding are crucial requirements for successful bookmaking. In this book all measurements given state the height by the length by the width (if applicable) in this order. Follow either metric or imperial measurements throughout.

cutting board and paper

Cutting chipboard can be hard work, as it is a dense board and needs repeated scoring. A sharp knife and non-slip backing on the straight-edge help avoid skidding and cut fingers. Hold the straight-edge down firmly with one hand and cut right up to the edge of the straight-edge, keeping the angle of the blade low and drawing it down in one clean stroke. Always work on a cutting mat. Paper, of course, is much easier to cut, but it is important to keep the blade low to avoid dragging the paper rather than cutting it.

It is essential that all papers, as well as boards, are used with the grain running in the same direction. Sticking paper with the grain in one direction onto a board with the grain running in another direction will result in a twisted board, which is impossible to correct. Unless otherwise instructed, cut all your board and paper with the grain direction running head to tail (i.e. running down the height parallel to the spine). You can determine the grain direction by lightly flexing the board or paper along both length and width. It will flex more easily with the grain.

sewing

Books are made up of either one single section or several sections (multi-section). With **single-section**

bindings the pages and the endpapers are all sewn together at once. Depending on the size of the book, you may need three, five or seven sewing stations. For five sewing stations divide the spine into six equal divisions and mark the five points with a pencil, both on the outside of the sections and on the inside.

Thread a needle with a piece of thread three times the length of the spine. Working from the inside, push the needle through the center mark to the outside (1), pull the thread through and leave a tail on the inside that is long enough to tie off later. Take the needle up to the next mark and push it back through to the inside. Take the needle up to the top mark and push back through to the outside. Then, go back down to the hole below and

①

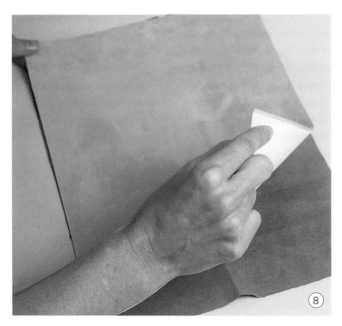

laminating

In some of these projects, one or two layers of paper and suede or vellum are stuck together to make a strong cover. The grain direction of all the pieces to be laminated must run in the same direction. If you follow the instructions above for glueing and always work on a clean surface, this should present no problems.

Have several sheets of clean newsprint to hand. Lay one of the pieces to be laminated on a sheet of newsprint and glue out the other piece on another clean sheet. Move the gluey newsprint well out of the way when it is finished with. Lift the glued sheet of paper (or suede or vellum) using finger and thumb at diagonally opposite corners so that the glued area faces down and can be positioned carefully over the other piece. Let one corner down, and gradually ease the glued surface across the other surface, smoothing out any wrinkles or creases as you go (8). When it is stuck down, rub down well through silicone paper with the flat of a bone folder. If another layer is to be stuck on, repeat the procedure.

corners

To turn corners in neatly when covering board with paper or material, use a pair of scissors to cut the paper or fabric across the corners (9). You may find it easier to bisect the right angle of the corner with a pencil line,

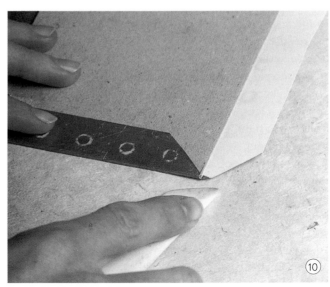

then draw a line perpendicular to that on the paper. You will now have a "T" shape. Cut the top of the "T" a little further out from the corner than the thickness of the board being used.

Glue the turn-ins, then turn the top and bottom edges in to the inside of the board, making sure there are no gaps along the edge. Tuck in the little piece at the corner with the bone folder (10). Turn the foredge in and use the bone folder to make sure the corner piece is tucked in neatly and stuck down well. Practice this technique with odd scraps of paper and board.

fastenings

There are many ways of keeping books or portfolios closed. Buttons and cords are used in several of the projects in this book.

To plait your own cord, use a buttonhole-weight polyester or silk thread, and cut nine lengths, each about twice the required finished length plus a little more. Knot the threads together at one end and secure them to a piece of wood with a thumbtack. Divide the threads into three strands of three threads each, and plait them to a little more than the desired length (11). The end can be tied off with a neat knot or secured with a bead. To fix the plait into the board, knock a hole through the board with an awl and, on the inside, cut out a narrow channel to take the thickness of the plaited threads. Untie the first knot and thread the plait through. Glue the end down into the channel you have made, and bang the hole closed using a hammer. This grips the cord and helps hold it in place.

Elastic loops can be used as fastenings by securing the loop into a board through a hole made with an awl, and glued down on the inside in a depression previously cut out. The elastic loop can slip over a bead or a piece of dowel or driftwood secured to the other board. If you want colored elastic, dye it by cutting off the required length and dropping it into a bottle of acrylic ink. Leave it submerged for at least 10 to 15 minutes, then pull it out with tweezers and leave to dry.

Using a strong linen or polyester thread (12), buttons can be sewn through holes made in the board with the awl. Do not pull the thread too tightly or you will pull the button down onto the surface of the board. Keep your sewing loose enough so that you leave a "stem," and wind the thread round and round this "stem" before taking the needle to the inside and tying off securely.

Make your own buttons by using a fine saw to cut slices from a length of broomhandle or a dowel for round buttons, or square-section pieces of wood for other shapes. If you want to color wooden buttons, do so by using acrylic inks, then polish them when the ink has thoroughly dried. Coconut shell makes beautiful buttons, too. Use sandpaper for a lovely smooth finish. Polish with wax polish. Finally, remember that found objects such as pieces of driftwood or small pebbles can also be used for closures.

proje

The following projects are not for people who want to repair old books: they are for those who want to create something new. They range from the simple to the advanced, and if you are new to bookbinding it would be sensible to begin at the beginning and work through each project, gaining confidence as you go.

Most of the books shown in the projects have blank pages, but there is no reason why they should not be adapted to bind an already printed book. Anyone who is reasonably dextrous and used to measuring and cutting accurately should be able to complete these projects. You may have attended a few classes, or you may be a complete beginner, but with care and attention to detail you should soon be able to produce your own books, whether to keep for yourself or to please your friends.

The projects can all be made with the minimum amount of equipment. A good-size work surface and a few tools, most of which can be bought from art supply and hardware stores, are the only essential requirements. The materials and dimensions for each of the projects are only suggestions. Once you have mastered the basic techniques so that they become second nature, let your imagination conjure up all kinds of ideas, and do not be afraid to experiment. Above all, enjoy your bookmaking.

handmade paper cover

SINGLE-SECTION BOOK SEWN ON TO A WOODEN DOWEL
designed by angela james

A single-section book is simple to make. Sheets of paper are gathered together and folded in half to make a single section. The number of sheets used can vary, but if you use thick paper, do not use too many, or the book will look clumsy. For the cover, select a suitable light card or heavy paper. If what you choose is not heavy enough, laminate two different papers together to obtain the required weight.

materials
1 sheet of heavy paper for the cover — measuring at least 370 x 560 mm (15 x 22 in)
4-6 sheets of plain text paper — 110 gsm would be suitable
1 sheet of contrasting or toning paper for the endpapers
400 mm (16 in) length of wooden dowel approximately 9 mm ($\frac{3}{8}$ in) diameter
acrylic ink, if staining wooden dowel
wax polish
1 m (39 in) thick natural linen thread

1 Cut the paper for the cover so that it measures 365 x 520 mm ($14\frac{3}{8}$ x $20\frac{1}{2}$ in). Fold in half along the long side, carefully matching the edges. Its dimensions should now be 365 x 260 mm ($14\frac{3}{8}$ x $10\frac{1}{4}$ in).

2 To form your single section, measure and cut the sheets of plain paper to the same height as the cover, but make the width marginally wider. Fold each sheet in half along the long side, matching the edges, then insert the sheets one inside the other.

3 Cut and fold the endpapers as in step 2 and wrap around the single section. Cut the edges to the same width as the cover with a knife and straight-edge (1).

4 Using dividers, mark the seven sewing stations down the center of the opened-out section of folded sheets by dividing the length of the spine into eight regular intervals, then prick through them with a strong needle. Mark the cover in the same way using a punch to take out neat holes of about 6 mm ($\frac{1}{4}$ in) diameter (2).

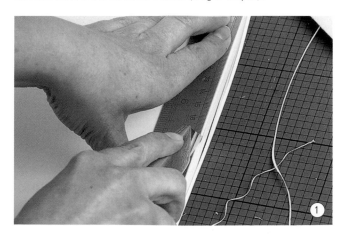

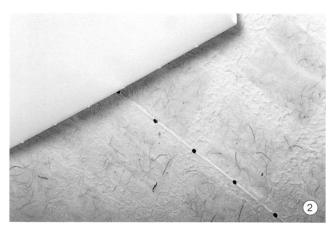

5 Cut a piece of dowel to the exact length of the spine. Smooth off each end squarely with fine sandpaper, sand the length of the wood to obtain a really smooth finish, and polish it with wax polish to bring up the grain and protect the wood. Alternatively, you could stain the

wood with acrylic ink, using a soft cloth to work the color in. When the ink is dry, polish as before.

6 The book is now ready to assemble. Cut a piece of linen thread about twice the length of the spine and pull it through a block of beeswax (3). Thread the needle. Place the section of folded sheets and endpapers inside the folded cover, lining up the sewing holes, and open out the whole. Starting from the bottom, push the needle through the first hole from inside to outside and through the hole in the cover, leaving a long enough thread end on the inside to tie off later. Place the dowel in position, against the spine, take the thread around it and go back through exactly the same hole to the inside. Take the needle up to the next hole, go through again and out of the cover, around the dowel and back through the same hole, pulling as firmly as you can. Continue this process (4), sewing up the book until you come to the last hole. Keep the tension the same all the way.

7 Tie off the thread on the inside of the section by looping the needle under the last stitch and through the resulting loop twice (5). Pull tightly and cut off the end to within 15 mm ($\frac{5}{8}$ in). Go back to the beginning and tie off the other end in the same way.

variation

The 2 books shown below were made using exactly the same technique, but different materials.

tip

i *f the sewing is pulled tightly enough, it should not slip on the dowel, but to make quite sure it stays in place you can cut a small groove on the dowel exactly at each point where the sewing thread will go around it. Use the dividers on the same setting to mark the intervals.*

casebound notebook

SINGLE-SECTION CASE BINDING
designed by angela james

This is another single-section book, but this time in a more traditional case binding, with a buckram spine and printed paper covers. When using buckram or bookcloth on the spine, try to find one with a good texture or weave. Some of them can be rather flat and dull. Also bear in mind that in time the edges will become rubbed and worn, so try to choose a fairly strong paper that is not too thick for the covers. The endpapers in this example have been printed to echo the outside cover, using the very simple method of dipping the edge of a pen top in acrylic paint.

materials
3 sheets of text paper or similar paper (90 gsm would be suitable)
$\frac{1}{2}$ sheet of contrasting paper for endpapers
1 piece of 1.2 mm ($\frac{1}{16}$ in)-thick grey chipboard, measuring 180 x 250 mm (7 x 10 in)
buckram or bookcloth 55 x 200 mm ($2\frac{1}{7}$ x 8 in)
$\frac{1}{2}$ sheet of patterned paper for the cover
linen thread
PVA adhesive
acrylic paint, if decorating endpapers

1 Cut 10 pieces of text paper measuring 145 x 205 mm ($5\frac{3}{4}$ x $8\frac{1}{8}$ in). You may add or subtract the number of sheets depending on the weight of paper used, but do not make the section too bulky. Fold all the papers together in half, keeping the edges lined up. Alternatively, fold each piece of paper individually, then insert one inside the other. They will be uneven on the foredge, but you can trim them once you have finished the sewing.

2 Cut two pieces of the contrasting paper to the same dimensions as the section papers; they will form the endpapers and the inside of the covers. If you are going to decorate them, do so now, then wrap them both around the section. If the paper is patterned, make sure that the two patterned sides face each other (1).

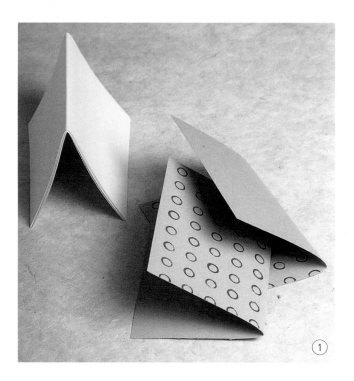

3 The sewing is simplicity itself. On the inside of the section, mark the middle of the center fold and then mark 55 mm ($2\frac{1}{4}$ in) above it and 55 mm ($2\frac{1}{4}$ in) below it. Make sure all the leaves are lined up and well tucked into each other, and pierce through the marks with a bodkin. Cut a piece of linen thread about three times the length of the pages, then wax and thread it.

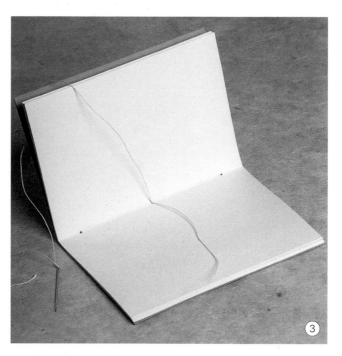

Beginning on the inside of the section, sew through the center hole and pull it out on the outside (2), leaving a tail inside that you will tie off later. With the thread now outside, go up to the next hole and push the needle back through to the inside. Skip the center hole and go through the other hole. From the outside, go back to the inside through the center hole, taking care not to catch the first thread. Pull the sewing very tight.

Open up the section. Have one end of the thread on one side of the sewing and one on the other, and tie off with a square knot (left over right and under, right over left and under), that will also tie in the long center stitch. Snip off the ends, leaving about 10 mm ($\frac{3}{8}$ in) of tail (3).

4 The foredge can now be evened up using a knife and straight-edge. Keep the ruler at right angles to the top and bottom, and hold the paper very firmly down when you cut so that the knife does not skid.

5 To make the case, cut two pieces of chipboard 150 x 100 mm (6 x 4 in). The boards should be about 5 mm ($\frac{1}{4}$ in) longer than the paper at both head and tail, and a fraction narrower from back to foredge.

6 Cut two pieces of patterned paper for the covers, each measuring 195 x 120 mm ($7\frac{3}{4}$ x 5 in).

7 Take the two pieces of board and the buckram and lay them out with the top edges of the boards in line with a distance of 12 mm ($\frac{1}{2}$ in) between them. Mark the position of the boards on the buckram with a pencil (4). Take the boards away and glue out the buckram. Reposition both boards on the buckram, ensuring that they are still in line at the top and that the distance between them is consistent all the way down.

While the glue is still wet, turn in the buckram at the head and tail (leaving no gap along the edges) and rub the whole area down with a bone folder (5).

8 Turn the cover boards over to the front and measure 93 mm ($3\frac{5}{8}$ in) in from each foredge. Mark the buckram and cut a straight line down, going over the edges onto the inside. Lift and peel away the excess (6).

9 Cut a good straight edge on one long side of one piece of patterned paper. Glue out the reverse side and with the case lying flat open on the table, outside up, carefully butt the straight edge of the paper up to the trimmed edge of the buckram, leaving no gap (7). Smooth down quickly with the side of your hand, pick up the case and, with scissors, cut across the corners of the paper 2 mm ($\frac{1}{8}$ in) away from the corner of the board (see page 14). Lay the case down flat again, inside up, and take the paper along the head and tail edges firmly over the edges and down onto the board. Tuck the two little corner pieces neatly in and bring the paper at the foredge over. Do the same on the other side. The whole procedure of putting down the sides has to be done quickly, before the glue dries, but it is not as daunting as it may seem at first.

10 To finish the case, set the dividers to a distance of about 20 mm ($\frac{3}{4}$ in) and run them around the three sides of each board to mark the turn-in margin. Cut along these marks with a knife and straight-edge, then lift and peel away the excess buckram and paper. *Do not* attempt to cut across the spine — the blade will almost certainly go through, which would be unfortunate. Stop at the edge of each board (8).

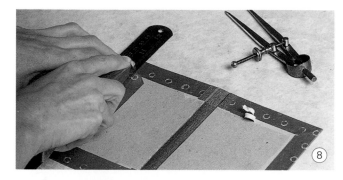

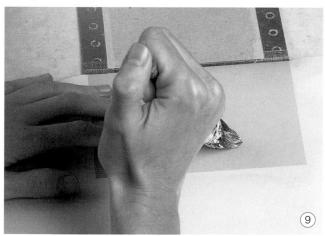

11 Lay the case flat, inside face up. Position the closed single-section on the right-hand board, right against the spine, with equal margins showing at head, tail and foredge. Slip a scrap sheet between the first and second endpapers and glue the top sheet thinly and evenly, brushing off the edges (9). Quickly and carefully take out the gluey scrap sheet and, without moving the position of the book, bring the other board up and over onto the glued paper. Open the board up again to make sure that the positioning is correct, make any slight adjustments before the glue dries, and then rub down with a bone folder through silicone release paper. Turn the book over and do the other side in the same way (10).

12 Slip a sheet of silicone paper between the boards and the endpapers, and leave the book between pressing boards for a short while to dry and settle.

multi-section variation

a multi-section book can be made in much the same way. Make up the required number of sections and make two endpapers by cutting and folding four folios of your chosen paper. Tuck one folio inside another to make two 2-folio sections. Sew the sections onto linen tapes, as shown on page 12, then place the book-block on the table with the spine just protruding over the edge. Hold the book down firmly, glue the spine with PVA adhesive* and stick a piece of linen down the spine, rubbing it down well with finger or bone folder. The linen should be just short of head and tail and be about 25 mm (1 in) wider than the spine on either side. The case is made in the same way as for the single section, but the spine, of course, must be wider.

Measure the width of the spine of the bookblock with dividers, and allow a further 12 mm (½ in). This should be the distance between your boards when you stick them down onto the buckram. Before the head and tail are turned in, stick a strip of card, exactly the width of the spine of the bookblock (use dividers to measure it) and the length of the boards, in the center of the buckram on the inside, with an equal gap between board and spine piece on both sides. Turn the buckram in and proceed in the same way as the single-section case.

*PVA adhesive is not recommended for gluing up the spines of more valuable books. Even so-called reversible PVA is not really reversible unless soaked in water, which will inevitably damage a book.

shades of blue

TWO-SECTION BOOK WITH "W" FOLD
designed by angela james

This book takes single-section binding a stage further. It is made up of two sections sewn through the cover using a "W" fold. The number of sections can be increased but, of course, the cover folds would also have to be increased to accommodate them. The design for the cover comprises torn squares from the linings of envelopes. You could use any patterned paper in the same way.

materials
3 sheets of medium-weight paper (100–120 gsm)
$2\frac{1}{2}$ sheets of colored paper for endpapers
1 sheet of watercolor paper (min. 300 gsm)
paper for collage
colored polyester thread
PVA adhesive

1 Begin by making the two sections. Cut six pieces of paper so that they measure 185 x 340 mm ($7\frac{1}{4}$ x $13\frac{3}{8}$ in). Fold each sheet exactly in half and make two sections with three folios each.

2 Cut two pieces of colored paper for the ends, the same height as the text pages but 10 mm ($\frac{3}{8}$ in) wider. In the example shown here, the endpapers are different shades of blue to echo the variation of blues on the cover. Line up the endpapers with the sections at the foredge and fold the extra width around the spine fold (1) so that when the book is sewn the thread will pass through the section and the endpaper together.

3 Cut a piece of watercolor paper to 185 mm x 370 mm ($7\frac{1}{4}$ x $14\frac{1}{2}$ in) i.e. the same height, but wider than the unfolded sections, to allow for the "W" fold. Measure and mark the center of the cover paper. Mark a vertical line down the center with the point of a bone folder and fold, matching long edges. Using dividers, mark 10 mm ($\frac{3}{8}$ in) either side of the center fold, mark a vertical line with the bone folder on both sides, and this time fold in the other direction to form the "W" fold (2).

materials

1 sheet of NOT or Rough watercolor paper (see page 10)
  300 gsm or heavier
2 sheets of NOT or Rough watercolor paper (185 gsm)
acrylic inks
200 x 100 mm (8 x 4 in) jaconette or linen
PVA adhesive
1 m (39 in) of double-sided satin ribbon 7 or 8 mm
  ($\frac{5}{16}$ in) wide
linen thread

1 Cut 12 pieces of the 185 gsm paper, 125 x 500 mm
(5 x 20 in). Fold each in half, lining up the short
edges. Wrap one folded sheet around another to make
six 2-folio sections (1). Cut one piece of the heavier
paper 170 x 600 mm (7 x 24 in) for the cover.

2 Soak the cover paper in a bath of cold water for at
least half an hour. Lift out of the bath and allow any
excess water to drip off before laying the paper on a
sheet of clean newsprint. Line up your chosen colors of
acrylic ink and, using the dropper in the screw top, drop
spots of color onto the wet paper (2). They will spread
immediately. When you have the effect you want, set
the paper aside to dry thoroughly. You can use a hair-
dryer to speed up the process, but this could move the
color around if the surface is still very wet.

3 Once the paper is dry, cut the height to 125 mm
(5 in). Fold to a width of 260 mm (10$\frac{1}{4}$ in) by marking
and scoring a vertical line using a straight-edge and bone
folder. Make sure the line is perpendicular to the long
edge. This will be the first spine fold. Mark the width of
the spine on the cover from the line of the first fold and
score a second fold line. The width is calculated by using
dividers to measure the thickness of the six sections one
on top of each other (3). Ensure that both fold lines are
exactly perpendicular to the long sides and parallel to
each other. Crease along both lines to make the spine (4).
Reinforce the spine by glueing a piece of jaconette or
linen 35 x 123 mm (1$\frac{1}{2}$ x 5 in) along the inside of it
and across the fold lines.

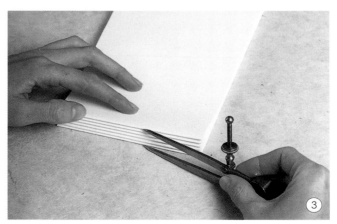

4 Set the cover aside and take the six folios of paper.
Line them up at the top edge and the spine and,
using dividers, work out the positions for the sewing

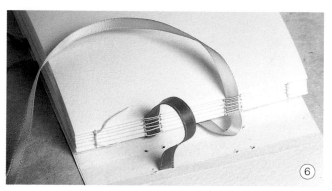

stations — 10 mm ($\frac{3}{8}$ in) in from either end to mark the kettle stitches, and 35 mm ($1\frac{1}{2}$ in) in from either end for the two ribbons. Then position the ribbons alongside the ribbon marks, and mark their width against the spine. You should now have six markings in total (5). For the ribbons, either cut a 1-meter (39 in) length of ribbon in half, or use two 50 cm (20 in) lengths of different color ribbons. Using a medium thickness linen thread (no.25/3 cord), sew the sections one by one onto the ribbons, following the instructions on pages 12 and 13. Tie off the loose ends at the start and finish with double knots.

5 Sit the sewn bookblock inside the folded cover, with the edges lined up and tucked well into the spine. Mark the position of each side of the ribbons on the inside of the spine. Remove the bookblock. Punch very small holes at either end of each ribbon position and cut between them with a knife to make slits.

6 Replace the bookblock inside the cover. Slide the ribbons through the slits to the outside (6). Tie the two pairs of ribbons in bows on the spine.

7 Finally, cut the foredges of the cover level with the pages, using a knife and a straight-edge.

The same technique has been used to make the book below, using unbleached linen tape together with a cover made from interesting Indian paper.

variation

leather-**bound**

POCKET BOOK
designed by angela james

This is a little book to tuck into your pocket for sketches or to use as a travel diary. It is made up of six sections, each consisting of six leaves, with endpapers at either end, sewn through the cover onto a strap that wraps around the book and fastens it. The cover is made of vellum laminated with suede, and the strap is a strip of leather laminated onto vellum. It is quite possible to increase the number of pages in this book by making more sections and allowing for a wider spine and a longer strap.

materials

3 sheets of text paper or similar
$\frac{1}{4}$ sheet of pink paper for endpapers
$\frac{1}{4}$ sheet of grey paper for endpapers
piece of vellum, at least 120 x 250 mm ($4\frac{3}{4}$ x $9\frac{3}{4}$ in)
piece of suede, at least 120 x 250 mm ($4\frac{3}{4}$ x $9\frac{3}{4}$ in)
piece of leather, at least 30 x 400 mm ($1\frac{1}{4}$ x 16 in)
PVA adhesive
black linen thread

1 Cut 18 pieces of cartridge paper measuring 100 x 200 mm (4 x 8 in) for the sections. Cut two pieces of pink and two pieces of grey paper to the same measurements for the endpapers.

2 Fold the text paper in groups of three sheets, matching the edges carefully, so that you end up with six sections with six folios each. Fold the endpapers, too — one pink leaf inside each grey. Set aside while you make the cover (1).

(1)

3 Make a template out of any old piece of paper about 115 x 215 mm ($4\frac{1}{2}$ x $8\frac{1}{2}$ in). Use this to cut out one piece of vellum and one piece of suede. Cut the vellum with the spine of the skin running in the same direction as the spine of the book.

4 Glue out the flesh side, i.e. the inside, of the vellum using PVA adhesive, and stick onto the inside of the suede. Make sure there are no wrinkles in the suede and then rub down thoroughly on the vellum side with a bone folder, paying particular attention to the edges. Put the laminated piece under a heavy weight between two boards and leave for 20 to 30 minutes. The edges at this stage will be uneven.

5 To make the strap, cut a strip of leather and a strip of vellum 30 x 360 mm ($1\frac{1}{4}$ x 14 in). Stick these two strips together in the same way as the cover and leave under a weight to dry.

6 Go back to the cover. Cut one of the long sides straight — do not cut any more than necessary, or you will not have enough height (2). Cut one of the short sides also, using a set-square to ensure a good right angle. Then cut the second long side so that the height is 103 mm (4 in). The other short side is left untouched and trimmed later, after the book is sewn. To mark the spine on the cover, measure from the foredge (the cut short side) 105 mm ($4\frac{1}{8}$ in) in, and mark lightly with a pencil. Using dividers, measure the thickness of the paper sections, holding them down lightly (it should be about 15 mm [$\frac{5}{8}$ in]). Mark this measurement on the

(2)

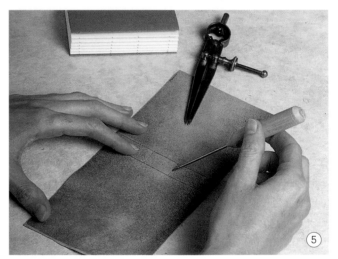

cover from the first pencil line (3). Use a set square to ensure a good right angle and mark firmly down each pencil line with the end of a bone folder to crease the spine folds.

7 Go back to the strap and cut it to the finished width of 23 mm (1 in). With the vellum cover on the outside, calculate the position of the strap on the spine, making sure that it is in the center with the same measurement on either side. Mark the spine lightly with a pencil on either side of the strap (4).

8 There are eight sections to be sewn through the cover (six white paper ones and two endpapers). Mark eight evenly-spaced points along the pencil lines on either side of the strap, and either pierce them through with a strong needle or use a very small punch (5). Mark the width of the strap on the spine of the book-block, as well as a kettle stitch mark 8 mm ($\frac{3}{8}$ in) in from either end.

9 To assemble the book, lay the cover on the table, suede side up, and place the first section, i.e. the endpaper section, against the first holes on the spine fold. Cut a piece of black linen thread 10 times the length of the spine, run it through beeswax and thread onto a needle. Open up the endpaper section and go through the fold of the paper with the needle from outside to inside at the first pencil mark (the kettle stitch

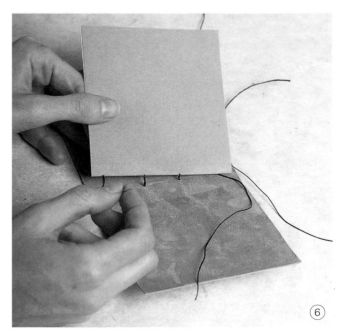

(7)

t is very important to keep the sewing tight throughout, or you will end up with a very sloppy book. As no adhesive is used, the book relies only on the sewing to hold it together.

note

mark). Pull the thread through, leaving about 100 mm (4 in) to tie off later. Come back through the fold and through the first hole in the cover to bring the needle out on the outside of the cover. Go back through the second hole on the cover and through to the inside of the endpaper, pulling the thread tight. Take the needle back through the endpaper at the other kettle stitch mark, but *not* through the cover again (6).

Insert the strap under the thread. One side should be the same length as or a little longer than the width of the front cover. The longer length is the back cover strap, which will wrap around to the front.

Lay the second section (the first white section) exactly on top of the first. Continuing sewing from the first section, take the needle through to the inside at the kettle stitch mark, keep the thread pulled tight, go along inside the fold and come back out and through the cover to the outside (7). Take the thread across the strap and back through the cover and paper again. Then go through to the outside of the section at the kettle stitch mark and add on section number three. This is sewn on in just the same way, coming out at the kettle stitch but

not through the cover at the end of each section. When you arrive at the end of the third section's sewing, the thread should be secured around the thread of the section below with a kettle stitch (see page 13). Do this at the end of every section's sewing from here onwards.

Continue sewing the sections one by one. The cover is gradually drawn up as it is sewn on. At the end of the last section, finish off with a double kettle stitch. Go back to the loose end at the start and tie that off around the section above it with a double kettle stitch (8).

10 Place a straight-edge between the pages and the cover, 1.5 mm ($\frac{1}{16}$ in) beyond the page edges to trim the cover. Hold firmly down with one hand while you cut. For the front cover, cut the strap separately at the same point. Trim the back foredge *but do be sure to keep the strap out of the way and not cut it.* The spare length of strap comes around from the back, across the foredge and onto the front and should be cut off 20 mm ($\frac{3}{4}$ in) short of the spine.

Cut to an inverted "V." The band that the strap slides through is made of a strip of leather 55 mm ($2\frac{1}{4}$ in) long and 8 mm ($\frac{3}{8}$ in) wide. It is wrapped around the strap and stuck with PVA adhesive on the underside (9). Place silicone paper and board on either side of this, put a weight on top and leave for at least half an hour.

(8)

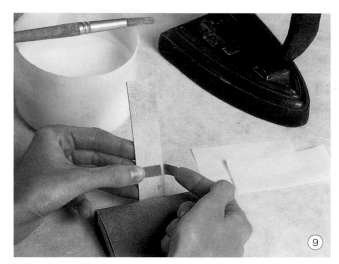

(9)

maple and suede

MULTI-SECTION BOOK WITH A WOODEN SPINE PIECE
designed by angela james

The book shown here has blank pages, but you could rebind any favorite volume in this way, provided it was in sections and could therefore be sewn properly. I have used two different colors of suede laminated onto each other for the cover. The spine piece is a thin strip of maple with drilled sewing holes. As each section is sewn, the thread goes through the cover and the wooden spine piece, so that the book is sewn and the cover attached all in one operation.

materials
10 sheets of text paper
1 sheet of a different color paper for endpapers
1 sheet of paper, white or colored, about 250 gsm
2 pieces of suede, each approximately 310 x 230 mm (12½ x 9 in)
wood measuring about 180 x 30 mm (7 x 1¼ in) and approximately 3 mm (⅛ in) thick
black linen thread
PVA adhesive
polish

(1)

1 Cut 28 pieces of text paper, each measuring 185 x 275 mm (7¼ x 10⅞ in). Cut two pieces of contrasting paper to the same size. Fold the sheets exactly in half, short edge to short edge, and make them into five sections, with six folios each, two of them with a contrast sheet around the outside (1).

2 Laminate the two pieces of suede, one on either side of the 250 gsm paper (see page 14) to make the cover, making quite sure there are no wrinkles on the suede. Rub down thoroughly, and if any glue gets onto the suede, remove it while still wet by wiping it with damp cotton and brushing up the nap once dry. Put the laminated suede between sheets of silicone release paper, with blotting paper on either side, and then between pressing boards. Leave it under a weight for approximately half an hour.

3 For the spine, measure a piece of wood to 18 mm (¾ in) wide and 155 mm (6⅛ in) long. Cut to size, making sure you have good straight edges. Depending on the wood used you may be able to cut it by repeatedly scoring with a sharp knife, or you may have to use a fine bladed saw. Sand all the edges and both sides, particularly the top side, which should be as smooth as you can make it.

4 Knock the sections of the book square and lay flat to the edge of the table. Put a weight on top to keep them in place. Use dividers to calculate the six sewing stations and divide the spine into seven sections

as follows: measure 35 mm (1⅜ in) from one end, then 16 mm (⅝ in) from there, then 30 mm (1¼ in) further, then another 16 mm (⅝ in), then another 30 mm (1¼ in) and finally 16 mm (⅝ in). Mark with a pencil, using a carpenter's square to make certain the marks are vertical. Prick each point through with a pin. Also mark and prick 10 mm (⅜ in) in from either end for the kettle stitches (2).

(2)

(3)

5 Keep the dividers on the same setting, and lightly mark on the wooden spine piece with a soft pencil where the sewing holes will be, omitting marks for the kettle stitches. Using a square, draw a line very lightly across the width of the wood at each sewing position. Using the dividers again, mark five points evenly along the six pencil lines. Clamp the wood, top side up, to the table with a piece of scrap wood beneath and scrap card under the clamp to prevent it marking the wood. Very carefully and accurately drill a hole with a 1.5 mm (¹⁄₃₂ in) drill bit at each of the points marked (3).

Sand again with fine sandpaper — the pencil marks will be sanded off. Using a soft cloth, work wax polish into the top surface and all four edges and buff to a shine. Alternatively, after sanding the wood can be stained with a commercial colored wood stain or with diluted acrylic ink, and then polished as before.

6 Take the pressed suede cover and cut one of the long edges straight with knife and straight-edge (4). Measure from that edge the head to tail measurement of the pages, plus an additional 4 mm (¼ in). Cut the second long edge to these markings so that the height of the cover is now cut to size, i.e. 189 mm (7½ in).

7 Cut a length of linen thread seven times the length of the spine and run it through the beeswax block. Thread onto a strong needle that will pass through the holes in the wood. Lay the open suede cover with the outside facing up, and place the wooden spine piece in the center, equidistant from head and tail. Prick through each of the holes in the spine piece with a bodkin, right through the full thickness.

Turn the suede over, inside facing up, and place the first section of paper on top, lining up the sewing stations

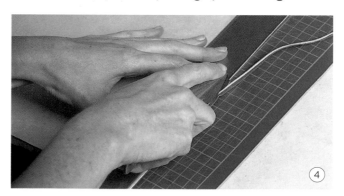

(4)

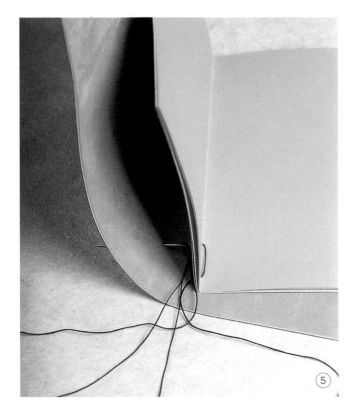

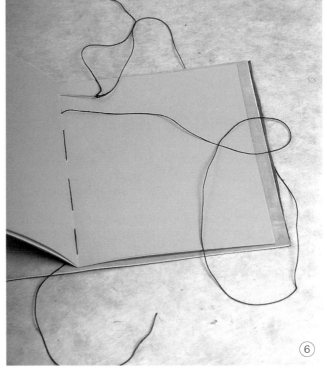

with the holes in the suede. Open the section up at the center. Put the threaded needle through the kettle stitch hole from outside to inside and pull through, leaving a tail of thread about 150 mm (6 in) long to tie off later. Push the needle back through the next mark, out to the back of the section and through the cover (5). Then take the needle through the first hole in the wooden spine piece. Move along to the first hole in the next row up the spine and push the needle back through the wood, the cover and the section to the inside. Push the needle through to the outside at the next point and, keeping the thread taut at all times, sew up the sections (6).

When you get to the top, take the needle out to the outside of the section through the kettle stitch hole, but *not* through the cover. Place the second section exactly on top of the first and sew back in the opposite direction. Once the third section is sewn on, secure it with a kettle stitch, and do this at the end of each line of sewing (7). It is awkward to slide the needle between the sections, but it is very important to keep the thread pulled tight or you will end up with a rather sloppy book. When the fifth and last section has been sewn on, tie off with a double kettle stitch. Go back to the tail of

thread left at the beginning and tie off in the same way. Snip the ends off to about 25 mm (1 in) and tuck them down into the spine.

8 To complete the binding, cut the foredges by placing a straight-edge between the bookblock and the suede cover, allowing a 3 mm ($\frac{1}{8}$ in) margin, and cut cleanly with a sharp knife. Brush the suede over and the book is finished.

spotty photograph
album

A ZIG-ZAG BINDING
designed by angela james

A zig-zag book is easy to make, provided it is folded very accurately. It can be as long or as short as you wish, though it will become unmanageable if it is too long. It need not be a photograph album. A zig-zag is a particularly good shape for children's books or for writing out a poem. This version is made using eight folds of lightweight card, the first and last pages being stuck onto the cover boards. When closed, the book is held together with two leather strips backed with Velcro. The board is covered with a watercolor paper onto which I glued spots of black Japanese paper. The paper is cut flush with the edges of the board, which have been painted with black acrylic ink and polished with beeswax.

materials
2 sheets of black, or black and white, card
PVA adhesive
1 piece of 200 x 200 mm (8 x 8 in), 2.3 mm ($\frac{1}{8}$ in)-thick
    chipboard
sandpaper
black acrylic ink
2 pieces of 200 x 200 mm (8 x 8 in) white textured
    paper, such as 190 gsm watercolor paper
$\frac{1}{4}$ sheet of black Japanese paper (Kozu or Mingei)
paste
40 x 200 mm ($1\frac{5}{8}$ x 8 in) black leather or black webbing
1 sheet white 90-110 gsm text paper
Velcro spots
1 sheet of black paper — 90 gsm text or similar
clear, all-purpose glue

1 For this project you can use either a black card or card that is black on one side and white on the other. Try to find one with the grain running shortgrain, i.e. the grain running with the shorter side of the card (along the height), as this will be more economical and will require fewer joins. Assuming this is what you are using, cut it lengthwise into three pieces measuring 175 x 555 mm (7 x 22$\frac{1}{2}$ in) each.

2 The three pieces of card will be folded to form the zig-zag. The fold lines must be exactly perpendicular to the long edge, and each folded face must fit exactly over the one below.

Starting from the left end of the first piece of card (black side up), measure in 175 mm (7 in) and mark a line down using a set-square and bone folder (1). Fold along this line, making sure the long edges are aligned. Slip a steel ruler under this first fold, the edge exactly in line with the foredge, mark a line with a bone folder and fold underneath along that line in the opposite direction, making certain that it is the same size as the first fold. Turn the card over, and mark and fold as before. There

1

will now be three folds and three pages, with a little bit left over. Measure, mark and fold the other two lengths of card in the same way.

Cut the leftover part of the first zig-zag back to 10 mm ($\frac{3}{8}$ in) wide. Glue thinly and evenly on the black side and stick the white side of the second zig-zag to it (2). Do the same with the leftover of zig-zag number two and stick zig-zag three to it. You should now have a concertina with nine sides. Cut the last one off with a knife and straight-edge, leaving eight equal sides in total.

3 Cut two pieces of chipboard so that they measure 180 x 180 mm ($7\frac{1}{4}$ x $7\frac{1}{4}$ in). Mark the grain direction on both pieces to ensure the paper you use later for covering the boards follows the same direction.

4 Find the center of one board by drawing diagonals from corner to corner. Measure a 45 mm ($1\frac{3}{4}$ in) square around it, and cut it out so that you have a hole right through the board. By making small holes at each corner with the awl you are less likely to overcut. Do this to one board only (3).

5 Using a fine sandpaper, sand the edges of both boards smooth, but do not round the corners. Paint all the edges with black acrylic ink. Allow to dry and apply a second coat. When that too is dry, rub the edges with beeswax and polish with a soft cloth. Try not to get beeswax on the sides of the boards, or you might have difficulty sticking the paper down later.

6 Take the black Japanese paper and tear out lots of spots about 20 mm ($\frac{3}{4}$ in) in diameter. With a fairly coarse sandpaper, sand the edges of each spot to make whiskers and, using paste, stick the spots onto the two pieces of white textured paper in a random pattern. Do not lose the whiskery edges. Rub them down through silicone paper with a bone folder (4).

7 Glue the reverse side of each spotty paper with PVA adhesive and stick down well onto each of the boards. Rub down through silicone paper and leave under a weight between boards and silicone paper for 15 minutes.

8 When quite dry, cut the excess paper off the edges of the boards, and also cut out the central square.

9 Cut two pieces of black leather (or webbing) 80 x 25 mm ($3\frac{1}{8}$ x 1 in). Take the board without the square hole in it, spotty side up, and measure 20 mm ($\frac{3}{4}$ in) in on opposite sides — the sides that follow the grain direction — exactly in the middle of the side, and draw a line 25 mm (1 in) long with that point at the center. Using a broad chisel and a hammer, make slots along the two lines, knocking the chisel through the full thickness of the board — put a thick piece of card or wood under it to protect your working surface (5). Turn the board over, and from each slot cut out a piece of board measuring 25 x 25 mm (1 x 1 in) and just deep enough to take the thickness of the leather.

10 Slip the pieces of leather through the slots so that 55 mm ($2\frac{1}{4}$ in) of it stays outside. Stick the leather that is left on the inside down into the depression you have cut out for it (6). Put the board on a hard surface — make sure you keep the white paper clean — and hammer the slot openings down to grip the leather.

11 Cut two pieces of white paper — text-weight would be fine — exactly the size of the boards, and stick them down on the inside of the boards (remember to follow the same grain direction!). Rub down well. *Do not* cut out the square in the center.

12 The boards can now be attached to the zig-zag pages. Put a sheet of newsprint under the first page and spread glue on the white side, off the edges — you do not want glue on the black surface (see page 13). Carefully line up the glued page on the board so that there is an even margin of white showing all the way around. Stick down firmly. Do the other side in the same way and make sure that the boards are aligned.

13 Cut a square of black paper to fit exactly inside the square cut-out and stick it in. You can then put a small photograph or whatever else you wish into the space.

14 Finally, stick black Velcro spots on the boards and on the underside of the leather strap with clear all-purpose glue (7).

i nstead of leather and Velcro, you could use ribbon, which you would slot through both front and back covers using the same method as for the leather.

note

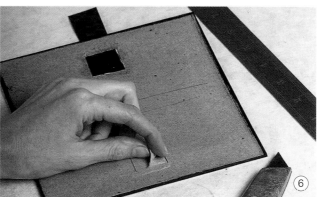

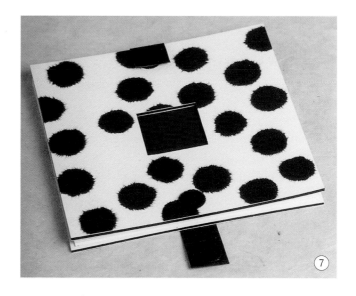

italian style

CROSSED-STRUCTURE BINDING
designed by angela james

This type of binding was devised and developed in Italy by Carmencho Arregui, and I am very grateful to her for allowing me to use it here. There are many variations of the crossed-structure binding. The one shown here is made from two pieces of vellum laminated together to make a sturdy cover. Careful measuring and cutting are essential, but once you have constructed one of these books successfully, you can play around with your own ideas.

materials
10 sheets of 760 x 350 mm (30 x 14 in) medium-weight
    paper, 110 gsm text paper would be suitable
paper for endpapers (optional)
2 pieces of 530 x 250 mm (21 x 10 in) vellum
or   vellum and one piece of heavy colored paper
PVA adhesive
linen thread
2 buttons (optional)

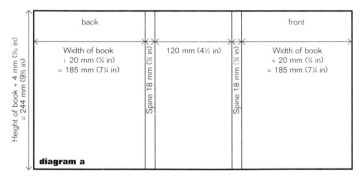

diagram a

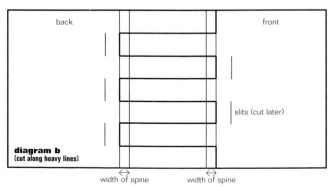

diagram b
[cut along heavy lines]

1 Cut and fold 28 pieces of paper measuring 330 x 240 mm (13 x $9\frac{1}{2}$ in) with the grain runnning head to tail. You should be able to cut three pieces from each full-size sheet if it is long grain (i.e. if the grain runs along the height), four if it is short grain. Fold into folios and make into seven sections with four folios each.

2 If you choose to have endpapers, cut two pieces of your selected paper to the same size as the other pages and fold each one in half. Alternatively, you could use two colors to match the vellums, cut two of each to size and tuck one inside the other.

3 To make the template for cutting the vellum cover, take a large sheet of paper and draw a vertical line down the right side. Measure 185 mm ($7\frac{1}{4}$ in) across and draw another vertical line. Measure the width of the book-block sections, which should be roughly 18 mm ($\frac{3}{4}$ in), and draw a third vertical. Draw another vertical line 120 mm ($4\frac{1}{2}$ in) further along, then another a spine width along, and finally a last vertical 185 mm ($7\frac{1}{4}$ in) on. You should end up with six vertical lines (see diagram a).
    Now rule a horizontal line across the top of the sheet at an exact right angle to the verticals. This is the top of the template. From this line measure down 244 mm ($9\frac{5}{8}$ in) and draw a horizontal at right angles to the verticals. This is the bottom of the template. Divide the central spine section equally into an odd number of sections (seven are shown here) and draw horizontal lines across (see diagram b).

4 Cut two pieces of vellum (with the spine of the skin running in the same direction as the spine of the book), a little bigger all around than the template. Glue the inside of one piece with PVA adhesive, covering thinly and evenly, and stick the two pieces together, inside to inside. Rub down very thoroughly with a bone folder and leave between boards under a weight.

5 When the vellum is dry, place it on a cutting mat, lay the template on top and secure it with drafting tape (1). Using a very sharp knife, cut precisely along the lines of the template — no slips or overcuts. You will probably find it easier at the inner corners if you first prick them through with a strong needle. This helps to stop the knife going too far. Lift off the template and there will now be two pieces of vellum cut out, one with three "fingers" and one with four (2).

6 You may decide to reverse one of the pieces of vellum (as shown here) so that the color of the back is different from the color of the front. The "fingers" should still fit neatly into one another. The three-finger

piece is the front cover. Lay this, inside upwards, on the table with the straps towards you. Lay the first section, or one endpaper, on top with the spine fold up to the edge of the cutaway. Leave an even margin at top and bottom.

7 The sewing on this book remains exposed, so use a durable thread such as linen or thick polyester. Cut a length 11 times the height of the spine, and wax and thread it. There is no need to mark up the backs of the sections for sewing, as long as you follow the positioning of the straps, but the kettle stitch positions ought to be marked, 10 mm ($\frac{1}{2}$ in) in from either end.

Go through the first section from outside to inside at the right-hand kettle stitch mark. Leave a 150 mm (6 in) tail of thread outside (3). Come back out exactly to the right-hand side of the first strap, take the thread across it and go back into the paper exactly to the left of the strap. Continue up the section, coming out and going in exactly on either side of each strap. This is important because if you make the sewing too tight it will pinch the strap in, too loose and it will not allow the back straps to fit in the spaces. Continue sewing each section on, forming the kettle stitch at either end and tying off with a double knot at start and finish. As with all the sewing described in this book, it is very important to keep an even tension on the thread (4).

8 Sit the back cover on top of the sewn book and allow the straps to pass between the ones on the front cover, fitting them snugly together. With a soft pencil, and keeping the straps parallel, mark the position where each strap falls, 20 mm ($\frac{3}{4}$ in) away from the spine edge on the opposite cover.

9 Place a cutting mat underneath the cover and punch a small hole on either side of the straps where you have just marked, except for the top and bottom straps, which do not slot through. Only five slits — two on the front and three on the back — are cut through the vellum covers for the other straps to slot through (5). Make sure the cuts are parallel to the spine and foredge. Slot the straps through to the inside. The top and bottom straps are cut a little beyond the line of the slits and are secured with buttons in this example, but a simple cross-stitch of linen thread would do the job just as well. Different ways can be found to make an interesting finish.

10 On the inside, the straps can be left as they are, or can be cut back to within 40 mm ($1\frac{1}{2}$ in) of the slits and glued down firmly with a clear general-purpose glue (6). Leave under a weight until thoroughly stuck.

11 Cut the foredge of the cover by placing a straight-edge between the pages and the cover, allowing a 3 mm ($\frac{1}{8}$ in) margin. Press down very firmly with one hand so that the ruler does not slip out of position and cut with a good sharp knife in one clean movement (7).

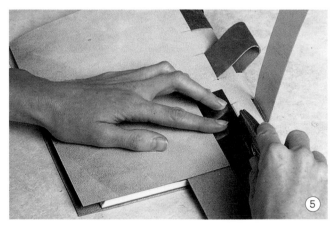

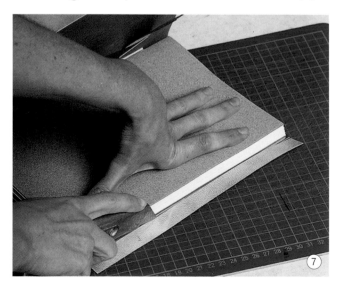

japanese octagon

TRIANGULAR BOOK
designed by angela james

This book is fun to make, and it surprises people when it is opened up to a big octagon. It can also be a good vehicle for calligraphy on the blank side. As with all the other projects, the secret of success is careful measuring and cutting. Choosing the right paper will also add to its final impact. The origami feel of the book suggested a Japanese hand-printed paper to me, but the choice is wide open. Clear a big space on the table when you start this project so that you have plenty of room to work.

materials
1 sheet of white card, measuring at least
    600 x 800 mm (24 x 32 in)
1 sheet of patterned paper, measuring at least
    600 x 800 mm (24 x 32 in)
1 piece of jaconette or linen, 250 x 400 mm (10 x 16 in)
PVA adhesive
newsprint for glueing on (not newspaper)
silicone release paper
silk thread
bead and button

1 Take the sheet of white card and draw on it a large circle 400 mm ($15\frac{3}{4}$ in) in diameter, using dividers or a lid to obtain a perfect circle. Draw a line through the center of the circle from one side to the other, i.e. the diameter. Draw a second diameter at exact right angles to the first to make four equal parts. Divide these four parts again to make eight equal segments. Take the ruler again, and this time draw lines from one mark on the circumference to the next to make triangles.

2 Lay the white card on top of the colored paper right side up and secure in a few places with drafting tape (1). Cut both card and paper together along all the pencil lines. Number each triangle lightly on the reverse with pencil along with its corresponding piece of colored paper so that if there is any slight variation, each piece will match anyway.

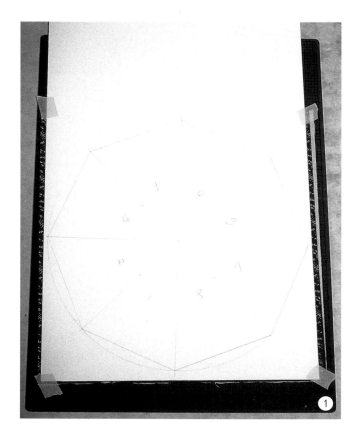

3 Cut seven strips of jaconette or linen 25 mm (1 in) wide and a little longer than the long edge of a triangle, i.e. 230 mm (9 in) long. Linen is much stronger, but the advantage of jaconette is that it is easier to cut and does not fray.

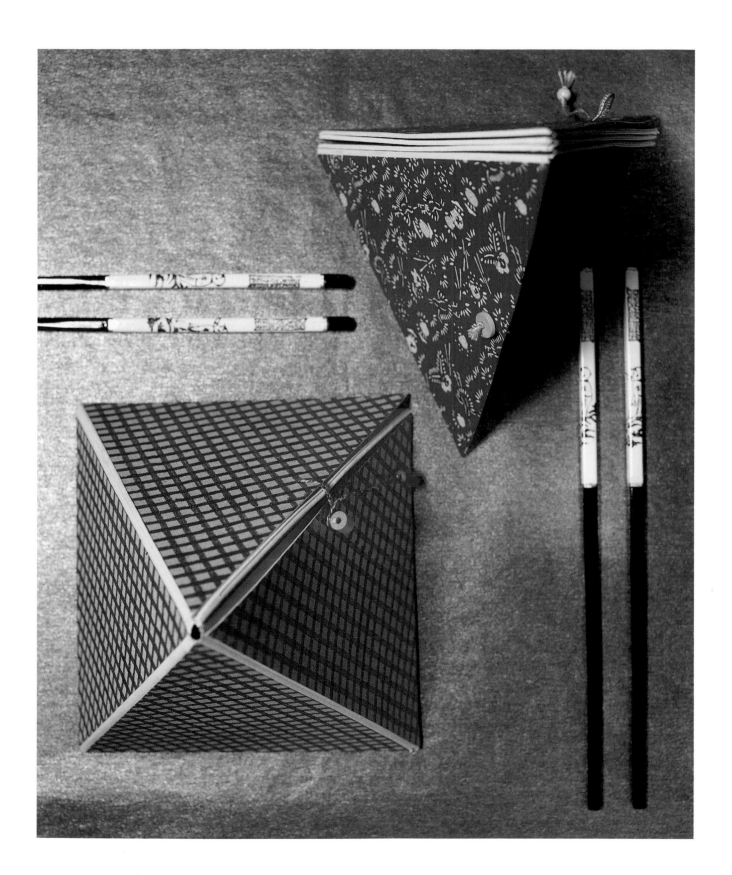

4 To assemble the triangular book, take the white card triangles 1 and 2. Using PVA adhesive, thinly apply glue to one strip of jaconette. Place glued side up on a piece of silicone release paper and lay the first triangle on it in line with one long edge and overlapping slightly less than halfway.

Lay the second triangle alongside the first on the glued strip, leaving a gap of 4 mm ($\frac{3}{10}$ in) between the two triangles. It is very important that the edges of each triangle run parallel and that the apexes are level. Turn the two triangles over and rub the jaconette down well with a bone folder over silicone paper.

Glue a second strip of fabric and stick one side down on the other long edge of triangle number 2. Triangle number 3 then sticks onto the other side of the fabric, again leaving a 4 mm ($\frac{3}{10}$ in) gap between triangles and lining them up accurately (2). Continue to join the triangles together in this way, but do not attach triangle

number 8 to triangle number 1 or you will not be able to fold the book up. As you work around you will probably find it easier to trim off the excess fabric at the apex before adding the next triangle (3). The excess at the bottom can be cut off at the end, using scissors or a knife to trim back exactly in line with the edge of the card.

5 Next, with the white octagon flat on the table, the jaconette hinge side up, stick the patterned paper triangles on. Each one is thinly glued on its reverse side and laid on top of its corresponding white triangle, carefully matching edges and apex. Rub down well with a bone folder through silicone release paper.

6 The triangles can now be folded alternately back and forward, so you end up with one triangular book with patterned paper sides facing out on both front and back (4).

(2)

(3)

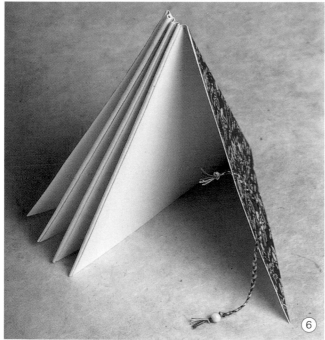

7 To make the fastening use a buttonhole thickness of silk or polyester thread matching or contrasting with the patterned paper. Cut nine lengths of about 240 mm (9½ in) each, knot them together at one end, secure them to a piece of wood with a thumbtack, then plait them to a length of about 130 mm (5 in) (see page 15) (5). Tie a knot at the end of it. Thread the loose strands through a small bead, tie another knot close up against the bead and cut off the remaining thread to leave a small tassel.

8 Using an awl, make a hole on the long edge of the back cover, and using a pin make a smaller hole on the front one, each the same distance up from the bottom or down from the top and 10 mm (½ in) in. Untie the starting knot of the plait, thread that end through the back hole and secure on the inside with a knot. Trim off the excess threads (6). Sew on a button or bead through the front hole, leaving enough of a stem of thread for the plaited cord to wind around. Secure on the inside again with a knot and trim off the leftover threads.

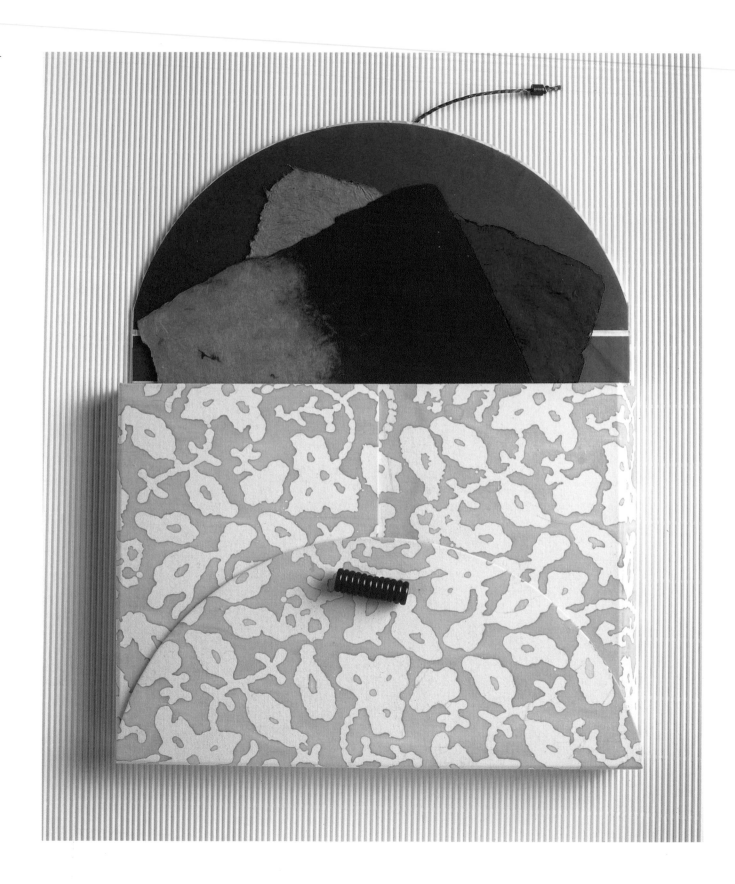

folding portfolio

PORTFOLIO STRUCTURE
designed by angela james

A portfolio can be used for any number of purposes. The case shown here is letter size, but you can make it as big or as small as you want it to be. For the covering I backed a cotton fabric with paper, but once again the choice of material is up to you. Buckram and bookcloth are easier to use and are inexpensive; leather requires some skill in paring to the required thickness. A sheet of rigid plastic could be used without the need for boards. It would be scored for folding, rather than cut into individual pieces and assembled. This portfolio is lined with paper. Depending on what use you have in mind for it, you could line it with felt, suede or another fabric. Bear in mind, though, that many fabrics fray and would, therefore, have to be turned in around a piece of card cut to size.

materials
lightweight fabric such as cotton or linen, measuring
    100 x 100 cm (40 x 40 in)
1 sheet of white paper, 800 x 620 mm (31 x 25 in) for
    lining the fabric, approximately 80–100 gsm weight
1 sheet of chipboard, 3 mm ($\frac{1}{8}$ in) thick
350 x 400 mm (14 x 16 in) linen, jaconette or bookcloth
PVA adhesive
cord and button
linen thread
colored paper for lining the inside

1 Lay the fabric out on a flat surface, inside facing upwards, and hold taut by placing weights at each corner. Place a large clean sheet of newsprint on another flat surface with the lining paper laid on top. Apply glue with a large brush, covering every area thinly and evenly. Overglueing will result in glue coming through the fabric and spoiling it. Without allowing the glue time to dry, carefully lift the paper up between finger and thumb at diagonally opposite corners so the glued side is upside down, and lay it down onto the fabric (1). Smooth it gently with the flat of your hand, turn over to check that there are no wrinkles, then turn back to the paper side and rub down with the flat of a bone folder.

2 Now cut all the pieces of board. There will be nine pieces altogether. Cut the first piece 3 mm ($\frac{3}{8}$ in) bigger all around than an $8\frac{1}{2}$ x 11 sheet of paper. Make sure all angles are right angles. This is your base. Cut a second piece of board exactly the same width but 2 mm ($\frac{1}{16}$ in) shorter than the base. Then cut this exactly in half

②

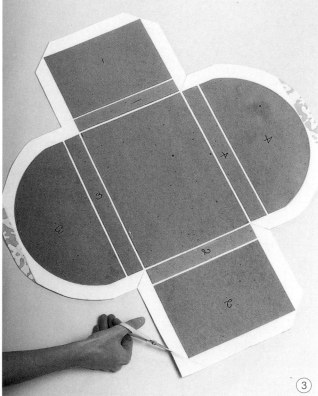

③

so that you end up with two pieces measuring the same width as the base board and 150 mm (6 in) in height. These are flaps 1 and 2. Cut two more pieces of board of exactly the length of the base, but two thirds of its width. These are flaps 3 and 4. Using a plate, cut these two flaps into curves on one side. Cut two further pieces of board, their length the same width as the base and 29 mm ($1\frac{3}{16}$ in) wide; these will be sides 1 and 2. Two other pieces of board, their length the same height as the base, one 31 mm ($1\frac{3}{8}$ in) wide and the other 33 mm ($1\frac{1}{4}$ in) wide, will be sides 3 and 4. Numbering the pieces will help when you come to assemble the portfolio.

3 The portfolio is now ready for assembly. Lay the pieces out on the paper side of the covering fabric, leaving an equal margin of fabric on all sides and a gap of 4 mm ($\frac{3}{16}$ in) between each piece (2). Mark around the base with a pencil and remove all the pieces and set aside.

4 Glue the base and place it inside the pencil lines. Rub down firmly, turn the whole piece over and rub down on the fabric side also, especially at the edges. Turn it back over and stick on the short sides 1 and 2 and flaps 1 and 2, remembering to leave the 4 mm ($\frac{3}{16}$ in) gap between each piece and to line up the edges — use a ruler to make sure they are in line. Do the same with the longer sides 3 and 4 and flaps 3 and 4.

5 Using a knife and straight-edge, cut off the excess fabric, leaving a margin of 30 mm ($1\frac{1}{4}$ in) all around for turning in. For the curved sides use scissors instead of a knife, and at the right angles cut at 45 degrees towards the corners of the base, cutting to within 3 mm ($\frac{1}{8}$ in) of the corner. For neat corners, the fabric at the top corners of the flaps should be cut as shown on page 14 (3).

6 Turn in the fabric, doing one flap at a time. Glue the three sides of spare fabric on side/flap 1. Stick them down well onto the board, pulling firmly over and making sure no gap is left along the edge. Stick the two sides in first and tuck the corners in neatly (see page 14) before sticking down the top edge. The turn-ins on flaps 3 and 4 should be snipped with scissors in "V" shapes, to within 4 mm ($\frac{3}{16}$ in) of the board, at intervals around the curve, before being glued and stuck down (4).

7 At this point, with knife and straight-edge, trim all the turn-ins so that they are neat, straight and at an equal distance in from the edge — if you are lining with paper rather than fabric, the line of the turn-ins shows through and it will look very much better if it is trimmed.

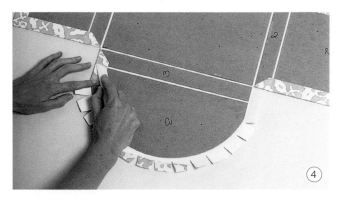

8 Cut four pieces of linen, jaconette or bookcloth 80 mm (3¼ in) wide. Two pieces must be cut to the length of sides 1 and 2 *minus* 4 mm (³⁄₁₆ in), and two pieces should be cut to the length of sides 3 and 4 *minus* 4 mm (³⁄₁₆ in).

Each piece is glued and stuck down on the inside of each side, across the gaps onto the base on one side and the flaps on the other. Do not push down into the gap when rubbing down, as this will inhibit the closing of the flaps (5).

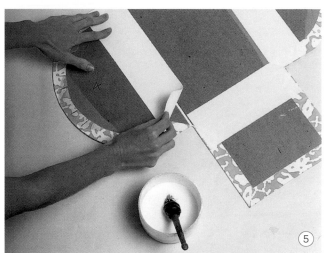

9 Close the portfolio — flaps 1 and 2 first, followed by flaps 3 and 4 on top. Mark the position on flap 4 for the cord that will wind around the button. On flap 3 mark the position where the button will be sewn.

Open up the portfolio again and use an awl and hammer to make a hole through flap 4 for the cord to be inserted. Cut out a small piece of chipboard on the inside for a depression to hold the thickness of the cord. Thread the cord through, glue down and hammer down the opening to close it up again and grip the cord. If possible, hammer on a hard unyielding surface such as metal or stone.

Finish off the other end of the cord with a knot or a bead. To attach the button, make two holes where marked on flap 3 and cut a depression between them on the inside to hold the thickness of the thread. Use a strong, waxed, linen thread, and sew the button leaving a stem; wind the thread around and take the needle through to the inside to finish off.

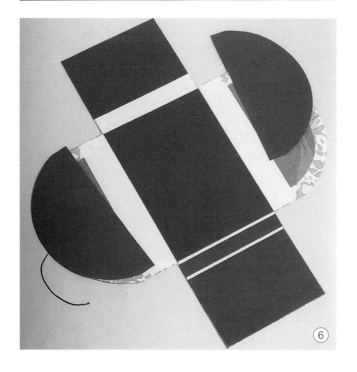

10 Cut nine pieces of your chosen lining paper, each 1 mm (¹⁄₃₂ in) shorter all around than the board sizes. Glue and stick each one, positioning it carefully and rubbing down well through silicone release paper to get rid of any creases there may be. Look out for any traces of glue on the surface. Should there be any, it should be wiped away immediately with dampened cotton before it dries (6).

wooden boards

SINGLE-SECTION BINDING WITH ARTICULATED WOODEN BOARDS
designed by peter jones

This binding was devised for a single-section text called "The Book of Nature," which measured 120 x 100 x 2 mm ($4\frac{3}{4}$ x 4 x $\frac{1}{16}$ in) prior to binding. The materials and dimensions for this project are given for guidance and refer to the particular completed binding shown. The method is adaptable to many different materials, sizes and formats, so the final constraint depends only on the imagination of the binder.

materials
2 sheets of white paper, 125 gsm would be suitable, measuring 125 x 210 mm (5 x $8\frac{1}{4}$ in)
2 sheets of colored paper of similar weight, measuring 125 x 210 mm (5 x $8\frac{1}{4}$ in)
1 piece of 4 mm ($\frac{3}{16}$ in) dowel, 135 mm ($5\frac{1}{4}$ in) long
carpet thread and buttonhole-weight thread
2 m (79 in) of stripwood, 15 mm ($\frac{5}{8}$ in) wide and 4 mm ($\frac{3}{16}$ in) thick
PVA adhesive

1 Fold the white sheets of paper in half along the length and tuck them into each other to form a section (1). Fold the colored sheets in half and wrap them around the section to form the endpapers. Trim all to the required size of 100 x 120 mm (4 x $4\frac{3}{4}$ in) and secure together with paper clips.

2 Open up the section and pierce four holes along the center fold for sewing stations at the following points: 12 mm ($\frac{1}{2}$ in) down from the head, 12 mm ($\frac{1}{2}$ in) down from that, 20 mm ($\frac{3}{4}$ in) up from the tail, 12 mm ($\frac{1}{2}$ in) up from that point (2).

3 Take the length of dowel and stain it black using waterproof ink. For the purposes of clarity the photographs of the book in the making show an unstained piece of dowel. As an alternative, you can use thin metal rod or tube available from model shops, carbon-fiber rod from kite specialists, or a kebab skewer.

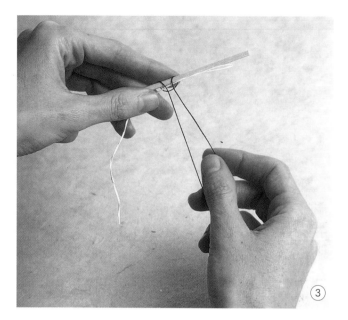

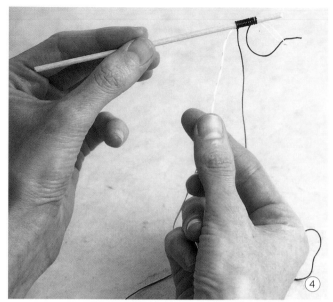

4 Cut a short length of buttonhole-weight thread and tie the ends together. Then cut a length of carpet thread six times the length of the rod, and with it form a hitch around the rod, leaving a length of 250 mm ($9\frac{3}{4}$ in) towards the head of the rod next to the head sewing station and the greater length towards the tail. (To form a hitch loop the thread, drape it over the rod, insert the ends through the loop and pull.) Then insert the loop of buttonhole thread between the hitch formed by the carpet thread and the rod, knot end towards the tail (3).

Using the shorter end of carpet thread, continue a series of alternating half hitches (i.e. one over and one under the rod) around the rod until you have built up a run of 12 mm ($\frac{1}{2}$ in) towards the head. The loop of buttonhole thread should be kept trapped along the length of the rod. Now insert the remaining short end of carpet thread into the loop of buttonhole thread and withdraw the loop back under the series of half hitches until you have pulled it all out (4). The short end of carpet thread is now secured under the half hitches.

5 Thread a needle onto the remaining long length of carpet thread. Sew into the hole pierced for the head sewing station and come back out of the section at the adjacent sewing hole. Form a hitch around the rod, ensuring the loop of thread formed inside the section remains taut (5). Take the needle back into the section at the same point and out at the third sewing station and

form another hitch around the rod. Take the needle back through the same sewing station, and come out at the the tail station. Form another hitch, trapping the buttonhole loop between this hitch and the rod. Again, make an alternating series of half hitches to build up a 20 mm ($\frac{3}{4}$ in) run and finish off as before, pulling the loop of buttonhole thread out (6). Align all the knots and dab them with diluted PVA adhesive to secure them. Trim the remaining tails of sewing thread at head and tail.

6 Cut 14 pieces of stripwood to a length of 135 mm (5$\frac{1}{4}$ in). I used a piercing saw to give randomness to the angle of these cuts and then stained the ends black. Place half of these pieces side by side, edges uppermost, ends aligned, and mark across the edges at positions just below the head and just above the tail sewing stations. The positions of these marks will ensure that the finished boards are properly located head to tail. Use a 1 mm drill bit through each strip from side to side at the marked positions (7).

7 Cut two lengths of carpet thread four times the width of the section. Bend each in half and form two hitches, one around the spine rod immediately below the head station, and one above the tail station, to give two pairs of thread tails. Form a square knot(s) (see page 12) if necessary to bring these tails up to the same plane as the holes through the stripwood. (I angled the holes through the strip of wood nearest to the spine.) Thread the strip of wood onto the two sets of paired tails (8) and form reef knots to secure it and space the next piece from it (9). Thread on the next, form a square knot, and so on until the foredge is reached. This should have used seven pieces of stripwood. Finish off with reef knots secured with diluted PVA adhesive and trim the thread ends.

8 Place the remaining pieces of stripwood side by side, edges uppermost, ends aligned, and mark the head and tail, except this time the holes will need to be drilled within the lines for the first board to allow for correct alignment of the hitches around the rod.

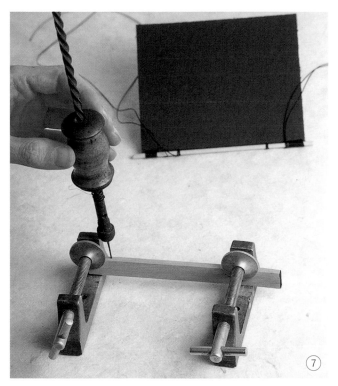

(7)

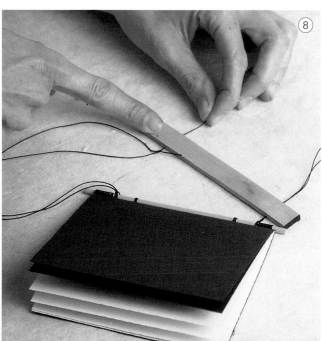

(8)

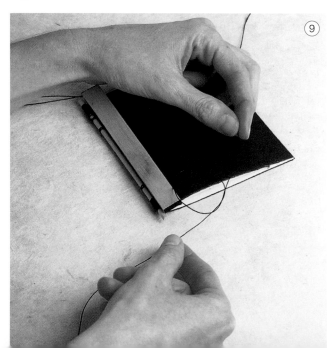

(9)

concertina book

DOUBLE-FOLD BOOK WITH PRINTED CONCERTINA
designed by sue doggett

This book is made from two interlocking concertina folds, with a supporting board at each end that can be covered in a plain or decorative paper. It was inspired by a structure by Julie Chen and Edward Hutchins, and it provides an ideal way to show off your artwork or your photographs. Almost any paper is suitable for the printed fold, but you will need a heavy paper for the support fold, to ensure that your book stands up. Proportions can be changed to suit your requirements.

materials

water-based block printing ink

glass, acrylic or acetate sheet

680 x 125 mm (27 x 5 in) paper strip for printed fold,
90–110 gsm would be suitable

watercolor pencils, paints

760 x 270 mm (30 x 10½ in) heavy paper strip for
support fold, 120 gsm would be suitable

PVA adhesive

2 pieces of chipboard for the cover, measuring
275 x 100 mm (10¾ x 4 in) and 1.5 mm (1/16 in) thick

1 sheet of plain or decorative cover paper, 90–110 gsm
would be suitable

1 Roll out the ink onto a smooth surface such as a piece
of glass, acrylic or acetate. Before printing, you can
draw into the ink using a pencil or paintbrush to vary the
texture. When you are happy with the design, take the
smaller strip of paper and lay it over the inked surface (1).
Rub down with the back of a spoon or with the back of
your hand. Then lift the paper carefully, making sure you
don't smudge the print, and leave overnight on a flat
surface to dry.

2 When the print is completely dry, you can work over
the ink with watercolor pencils or paint (2).
Alternatively, you can collage text, small illustrations or
scraps of colored paper to achieve your final image.

3 The next step is to fold the printed strip into a
concertina. To do this, first measure 50 mm (2 in) in
from both ends. Score with a steel ruler and bone folder,
then crease (3).

4 Fold the central section of the strip in half. Open out
again and then fold each half in half again (into the
center); this will give you four folds. Finally, fold each
of the four central sections in half again, making a total
of eight equally sized sections plus the shorter folds,
10 folds in total.

5 Take the heavier paper strip and fold into eight
equally sized folds (use the same method as above,
omitting the shorter end folds). You will now have two
concertina folds with which to construct your book (4),
by inserting one into the other.

(4)

(5)

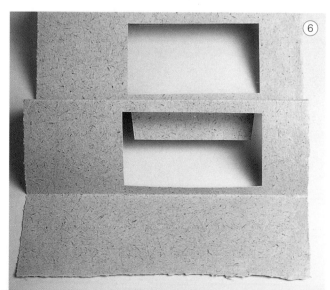

(6)

(7)

6 Put the printed concertina to one side and prepare the support fold as follows. On each of the folds except the outer two (which form part of the cover), measure 45 mm (1¾ in) in from the top edge, 10 mm (⅜ in) in from each side, and 95 mm (3¾ in) up from the bottom. To form a rectangular window on the six folds, mark each corner with a point of a needle or a pair of dividers. Make sure that the pin holes are aligned on each of the folds.

7 On the even marked folds only, using the pin holes as a guide, cut out the window completely.

8 The windows on the odd marked folds will form the supports for your printed concertina and they should be cut as follows: leaving the edge of the rectangle on the left-hand side of the fold intact, cut the other three sides to form a flap (5).

9 Divide each of the folds in half, score with a steel ruler and a bone folder, crease and bend towards the back of the book (6).

10 Measure 10 mm (⅜ in) down from the top right-hand corner of each folded flap. Using a steel ruler, line up this mark with the top corner of the uncut edge of the flap. Cut away this triangle of paper on each flap and then repeat on the bottom edges. The folds of the book are now ready to be joined together.

11 Apply PVA adhesive to the reversed half of the first window flap of the support fold (7). Carefully pull the printed concertina through the windows from the right-hand side until the right-hand edge of the third cut fold is lined up exactly with the edge of the glued window flap and centered within the window. You may find it easier to line up if you turn the book over.

12 Carefully pulling the printed fold through the windows from left to right, repeat the glueing process on the remaining two flaps, making sure that you glue the fifth fold to the second flap and the seventh fold to the third flap. Line up the printed folds centered within the window as before (8).

13 Fold up the concertina construction carefully and leave under a weighted board to dry.

14 Open up one of the cover folds to reveal an unglued end fold of the printed concertina. Open this out and place scrap paper in position (9).

15 Using PVA adhesive, glue the back of this end fold carefully. Remove the scrap paper and refold. Place a clean sheet of scrap underneath the glued fold as protection. Bring the cover fold of the support concertina over and close, rubbing down well. Remove the scrap paper and repeat this process at the other end of the book.

16 Cut two pieces of chipboard slightly larger on all four sides than the folded book and cover with your chosen paper. Trim, cut the corners and turn in (see page 14).

17 Finally, glue both ends of the completed concertina to the cover boards. To do this place scrap paper under the end fold of the book and glue, using PVA adhesive (10).

(8)

(9)

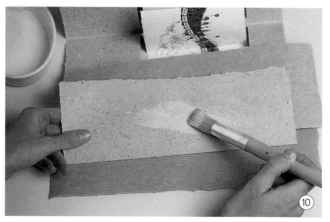

(10)

fuchsia star book

SEVEN-POINTED BINDING
designed by jeanette koch

A few years ago Vicki Jacobs left detailed instructions on the Internet on how to make a star book. The idea appealed greatly, and so all credit to Vicki for her simple method, which I have used and adapted to great effect and enjoyment ever since. The book is a seven-pointed star structure made of three different sizes of paper. Once you are familiar with the process, you can adapt it endlessly.

materials

3 sheets of colored paper, between 90–110 gsm,
    measuring 500 x 700 mm (20 x 28 in)
2 pieces of 1 mm ($\frac{1}{32}$ in)-thick chipboard, measuring
    50 x 150 mm (6 x 6 in)
polyester buttonhole-weight thread
2 sheets of handmade plant paper, 150 x 150 mm
    (6 x 6 in), to cover the boards
500 mm (20 in) of fastening (double-sided ribbon,
    plaited thread, or cord)

1 For this project, color A is magenta, B is blue and C is orange.
Color A: cut seven pieces, 100 x 200 mm (4 x 8 in)
Color B: cut seven pieces, 200 x 50 mm (8 x 2 in)
Color C: cut seven pieces, 200 x 150 mm (8 x 6 in)

2 Fold all seven A pieces in half, to make a square. Fold all seven B pieces in half along the longer side, and in half again along the shorter side. Their dimensions should now be 100 x 25 mm (4 x 1 in). The short, folded edges are now the top of pieces B. Mark a light pencil star near the top left-hand corner of each piece B.

3 Using a bone folder, make a light, horizontal crease across the middle of each C piece, having folded it gently along its longer side. Open up the piece. Using dividers, mark 5 mm ($\frac{1}{4}$ in) in from the bottom left-hand corner, and 5 mm ($\frac{1}{4}$ in) in along the horizontal crease. Do the same on the right-hand side. With a craft knife and a straight-edge, and using the marks made with your dividers to guide you, cut out two 5 mm ($\frac{1}{4}$ in)-wide strips of paper, from the bottom of the paper up to the half-way crease, on both the right- and left-hand side. You now have a T-shaped piece of paper. With the "T" the right way up, fold the paper in half, bottom to top, and then in half again left to right. You now have a rectangular piece, with the cutaway sections on the inside. Note: If you want to draw or write anything in the starbook, now is the time to do so (1).

4 Stack up all seven A pieces, with the folded edges all facing the same way and exactly aligned. Put them between pressing boards so that the folded edges line up with the edges of the pressing boards and weigh down. Using dividers and a pencil, divide the spine equally into five 20 mm ($\frac{4}{5}$ in) intervals, and mark four lines across the spine. These are your sewing stations.

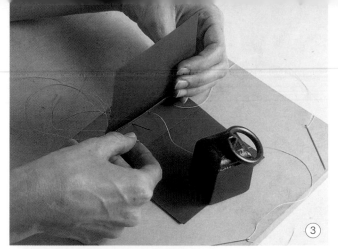

(2)

(3)

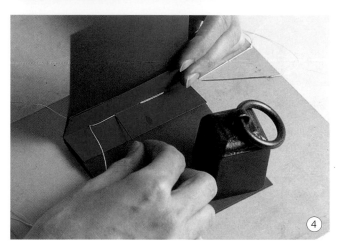

(4)

5 Remove from the pressing boards. With the fold on the left-hand side, mark a light pencil star in the top left-hand corner of each A piece.

6 Using a toothpick, spread a strand of PVA adhesive along the spine of one folded piece B and fit it snugly into the fold of one piece A, with the folded short end at the top. Your pencil star mark should be at the top of each piece. This is your AB unit (2). Repeat to make seven AB units. Stack the seven units evenly and place them between blotting paper and your pressing boards with a weight on top. Leave to dry.

7 The outside fold of each AB unit shows the four sewing stations marked in step 4. Measure and mark the same sewing stations on the inside fold of each AB unit. Use a pin to push through from the inside to the outside mark. Do this carefully, so that your pin emerges exactly through the sewing hole marks made on the A pieces in step 4.

8 Take your thread and cut it into two equal lengths: thread A and thread B. Take four needles, and thread a needle on to each end of thread A and thread B. Take thread A, and insert one needle into the top stitching hole, pushing from the inside to the outside. Take the needle on the other end of thread A and push through sewing hole 2, again from the inside to the outside. Pull the thread taut and even out the lengths. Repeat with thread B and sewing holes 3 and 4. Thread A and thread B work independently of each other throughout the sewing up (3).

Take the next AB unit (remembering to check that your pencil star is at the top) and insert your first needle (from thread A) into corresponding sewing hole 1 of this unit, but this time pushing from the outside to the inside. Insert the second needle into sewing hole 2 and pull taut. Take the needle from sewing hole 1 and push back out through hole 2, making sure that you do not push your needle through the thread. Take the needle from sewing hole 2 and push it back out through sewing hole 1. Repeat this process with thread B and sewing holes 3 and 4 (4).

Repeat this procedure until you get to your last AB unit, making sure that you keep your sewing taut and even. When you reach the last (seventh) unit, push all the needles in through their respective sewing holes. Knot together the threads of holes 1 and 2, and do the same for the threads of holes 3 and 4, checking that they are firmly knotted and taut against the inside fold before cutting the spare threads away neatly against the knots.

9 Now add the C pieces to the book. Piece C should fit snugly in front of the fold of piece B. Line up the outside edges so that the spine of the C piece lies just outside the edges of the B piece. Its folded edge must be at the top, matching piece B. You may have to trim the outer edge slightly to achieve a perfect fit. Using PVA

adhesive and a small brush, glue a strip about 5 mm ($\frac{1}{4}$ in) wide down the outer edges of piece C, and stick to the inside edge of piece A. Repeat with the remaining six C pieces (5).

10 Now glue the outer edges of the A pieces together, except for the outermost sides, which will eventually be attached to the cover boards (i.e. glue six pairs of outer edges together in total). Using PVA adhesive, glue a strip about 5 mm ($\frac{1}{4}$ in) wide along the outer edge of an A piece, and stick to the outer edge of the next A piece.

11 Place the book between blotting paper and pressing boards with a weight on top. Leave to dry for about 15 minutes.

12 Cut two pieces of chipboard slightly larger than the dimensions of your book, making sure that the grain runs from top to bottom. Place the closed star book on one of the pieces, and mark carefully around the edge of the book. Square up the outline. Cut the two boards and check again that they are equal in size and perfectly square. Using sandpaper, lightly remove the sharp edges, but do not round off the corners.

13 Cut out two oversize pieces of covering paper. Lay one cover board on the wrong side of the first piece. Using a soft pencil, mark the outline of the board on the paper. With PVA adhesive, glue one side of the board and place it on the pencilled outline. Turn the board over and rub the paper down well, using a bone folder through a sheet of silicone paper. Place the board between clean paper and pressing boards, with a weight on top. Leave it to dry while you repeat the process with the second cover board.

14 When the cover boards are dry, mark your turn-ins on the paper. Using dividers, mark a 10 mm ($\frac{1}{2}$ in) border on the pieces of paper, all the way around the boards. Cut the excess paper away. Fold in the corners of your cover paper as explained on page 14. Rub down well through silicone paper and leave under pressing boards and a weight to dry while you repeat the process with the second cover board.

15 When both boards are dry, measure the width of your ribbon or fastening, mark the appropriate size vertically 10 mm ($\frac{1}{2}$ in) in from each cover board edge, and centered between the top and bottom edges. Take a chisel the same width as the ribbon, position it along the marked slot and hammer it through the cover board (6). Thread the ribbon through the slot. Turn the board over and, making sure the ribbon is flat and straight, hammer closed the lip of the chisel hole. You should end up with a flat surface and your ribbon gripped firmly in position. Repeat with the second cover board.

16 Make a precise and careful cut around the ribbon ends lying inside your cover boards. Peel back a thin layer of card to create a recess. Glue the recess and stick the ribbon down into it.

17 Wrap the fastenings in a piece of plastic bag to protect them. Then, using PVA adhesive, glue the inside of one cover, right up to the edges; glue one of the outer sides of your star book. Ensure that the whole surface is covered, but do not overglue. Make sure the book is the right way up, then place it down squarely on the cover. Rub down well through silicone paper. Do the same for the second cover and the other side of the book. Put the book between paper and pressing boards and under a weight until completely dry.

contemporary book bindings

Bookbinding is a traditional craft, but modern bookbinders combine both old and new techniques and materials to produce contemporary bindings that form not only a protective covering for the book but also a unique work of art. The following pages include a selection of bindings by book artists from around the world, demonstrating a diverse range of styles and treatments.

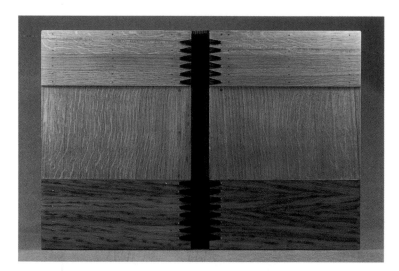

P.R. JONES
"Cite Corsan's"
1997; 279 x 198 mm
Sewn on carbon fiber spine rods. Boards of coarse sawn oak with oak cross strips riveted down with copper rivets.

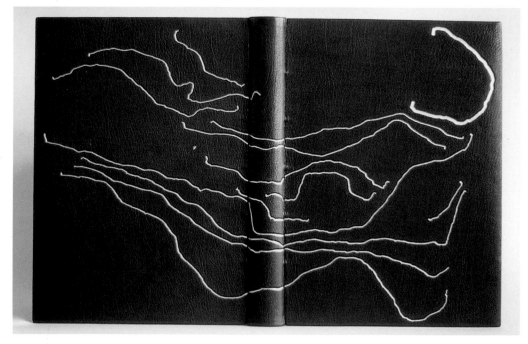

IVOR ROBINSON
"The Sonnets," Shakespeare
1992; 270 x 190 mm
Black goatskin tooled in gold. The binder has attempted to retain the immediacy of drawing through the gold impression on the leather. It presents a comparable personal and autographic quality.

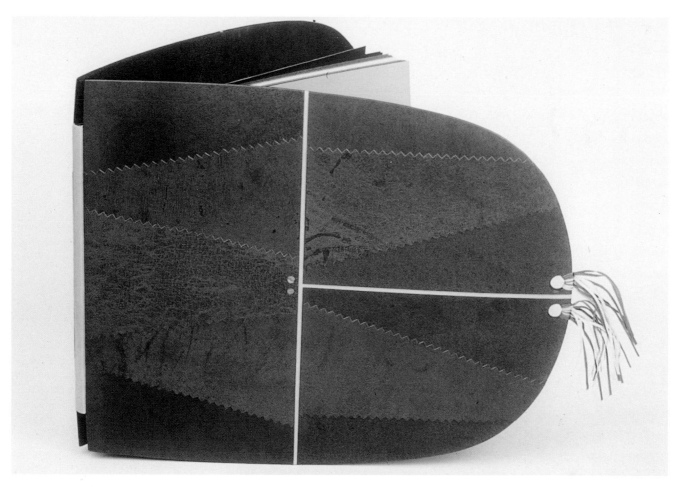

SUN EVRARD
"De la Sainte Famille au
Droit à la Paresse," Rene Char
1993; 280 x 230 x 10 mm
*Simplified binding in
yellow box calf and violet
kangaroo skin, with leather
thongs and doublures.*

ANGELA JAMES
"The Left Handed Punch"
1997; 392 x 294 mm
Detail of front board.
*Acrylic-colored calf and
paintings under transparent vellum.
Moveable Punch and Judy figures.*

MARK AND MIDORI COCKRAM
"Yamato-Toji"
1999; 200 x 150 mm
*Bound in kimono silk, with
silk ribbon ties. Handmade
Japanese paper bookblock.
Title strip with Japanese
calligraphy.*

HEDI KYLE
"Train Log"
1996; 165 x 152 x 50 mm
*Crimped exotic paper, leather, Firenze
paper soaked in coffee and painted,
waxed linen thread, Amtrak paper
towels, wooden stick covered with
Japanese paper, colored pencil writing,
computer generated text rolled up.
Codex and scroll formats.*
photo credit to: Paul Warchol

PHILIP SMITH
"Visual and Verbal Contemplations"
1987; books: 109 x 74 x 12 mm,
container: 380 x 267 x 23 mm
Transparent book-form container with nine
small books sewn on colored threads to
expose section folds. Painted with an overall
image of an open book on the front covers.
photo credit to: Michael Barnett

PHILIP SMITH
"L'Infinito," Giacomo Leopardi
1997-8; 324 x 246 x 35 mm
A "simulated maril" binding in a LapBack
structure. This variant is a LapBack with three
yokes; the longer central one has the title
stamped in black. The upper laminars of the board
are sculptured with a low relief book-winged
figure in geometric form. The boards are covered
in cotton calico with an undercoat of white
emulsion and overpainted with acrylic colors.
photo credit to: Philip Smith

TIMOTHY C. ELY
"Secret Passage One"
1989; 241 x 285 mm
Pigment, paste and resin
on Barcham Green paper.
Sewn on tapes with a
hollow back, leather
joints and Japanese
paper in the endpapers.
Two-tier silk endbands.
The whole book was
blind tooled.

TREVOR JONES
"Urne Buriall and Garden of Cyrus," Sir Thomas Browne
1996; 321 x 235 mm
The binding is covered in natural "Archival" calf with dyed areas, using stencils and resists, and inlays and sunk onlays of calf and goatskin. Starch-grained endpapers designed and made by the binder. All edges were gilt in the rough over red Armenian bole with random patches of palladium before sewing. The grey goatskin doublures are blind tooled. The book-style box is covered in art buckram, with reversed-leather suede and felt linings and a leather label.
photo credit to: Trevor Jones

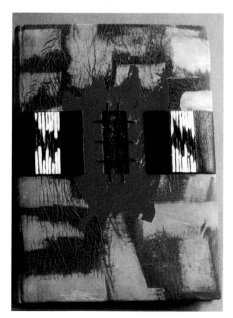

DAVID SELLARS
"The Restraint of Beasts," Magnus Mills
1998; 220 x 155 mm
Full binding in prepared goatskin, feathered red onlays, raised board area covered with black goatskin inlaid with burnt matchsticks and emulsified leather dust. Recessed cutaway area of front board contains emulsified leather sculpture.

DAVID SELLARS
"Hamlet," William Shakespeare
1998; 350 x 230 mm
Tongue-in-slot structure, covered in various leathers, vellum recessed panel, exposed sewing over raised elements, title onlaid and tooled vellum.

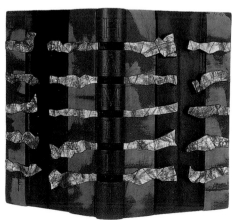

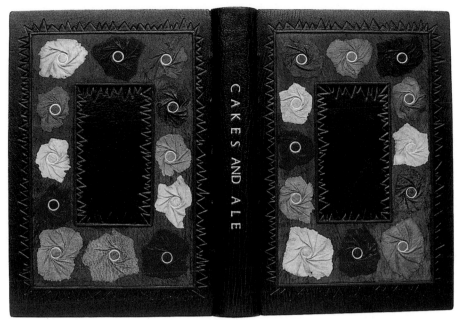

SALLY LOU SMITH
"Cakes and Ale,"
W. Somerset Maugham
1996; 232 x 156 mm
*Covered in dark green goatskin
and inlaid with sanded dark green
goatskin. Onlaid with crumpled
goatskin in greens, pinks and
reds. With gold and blind tooling.*

JAMES BROCKMAN
"The Van," Roddy Doyle
1991; 195 x 130 x 38 mm
*Bound in full natural calf over
sculptured boards with recessed
"van" fragments (rusty metal,
plastic trim etc.) The calf was air-
brushed with leather dyes and
lettered using metallic foils. The
edges were decorated with a
tire tread design. The doublures
and fly-leaves were lined with
gingham and wood grain fablon
stained with egg, ketchup colors
and decorated with a collage of
food wrappers.*

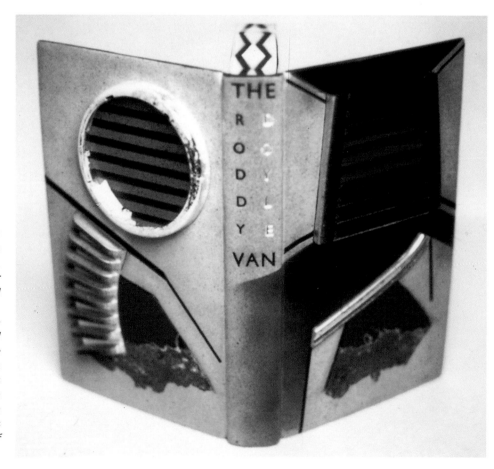

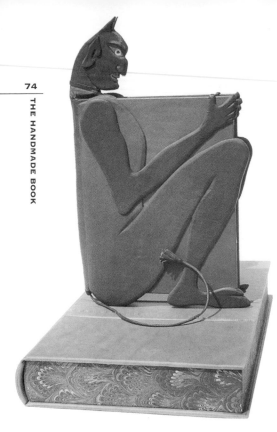

JAN B. SOBOTA
"Rimska Lyrika" (The Lyric
of the Roman Empire)
1987; book: 250 x 25 mm,
stand: 270 x 270 x 70 mm
*Natural calfskin, blind
tooling, decorative edges
and headbands. Stand
made with board, balsa
wood, natural goatskin,
dark red calfskin onlays.*

JAN B. SOBOTA
"L'Heritier du Diable"
1990; 365 x 220 x 30 mm
*Book sculpture — board, blue, dark
blue and brown roughly fabricated
calfskin. Sitting devil with a moveable
head. Pulling the devil's tail when the
book is closed causes him to bend his
head downward. As the book opens
the devil raises his head slowly.*

MANNE DAHLSTEDT
"Aniara," Harry Martinson
1997; 240 x 160 mm
*The book is sewn on steel rings
with covers of sheet metal.*
(owned by The Royal Library, Stockholm)

JEFF CLEMENTS
"Rime," Boccaccio
1986; 260 x 140 x 25 mm
Covered with a series of
inlaid areas of goatskin, in
beige, red, grey, dark
green, orange and blue.
The lines are blind tooled.

JENNI GREY
"The August Sleepwalker," Bei Dao
circa 1990; 210 x 130 mm
Wrap-around style of binding in
red and black dyed vellum, with a
wooden clasp stained black.

JENNI GREY
"The Essence of the Thing,"
Madeline St. John
1997; 200 x 130 mm
Leather spine with boards
covered in "fiddleback" veneer
and blackened brass arrowheads.

index

Page numbers in *italics* refer to illustrations.